WHAT MAKES A SAINT?

The story of twenty-five famous men and women

Patricia Keefe

WHAT MAKES A SAINT?

The story of twenty-five famous men and women

SCEPTER

London – New York

This edition of *What makes a Saint?* is published:
in England by Scepter, 1 Leopold Road, London W5 3PB; and
in the United States by Scepter Publishers Inc., 481 Main Street,
    New Rochelle, N.Y. 10801.

British Library Cataloguing in Publication Data
Keefe, Patricia Mary *1939 –*
    What makes a Saint?
    1. Saints.
    I. Title
    270.092

    ISBN 0 906138 30 2

Cover design and typeset by KIP Intermedia and printed in
Singapore.

Contents

FOREWORD

What is the common denominator which makes Saints from ordinary people of such diverse ages, races, backgrounds and talents? Some had the good fortune to be born into a practising Catholic family. Others found their way to the Church after a long spiritual journey. Some attained sanctity while still very young, others after a long life on earth. But each one, in his or her own circumstances, strove wholeheartedly *to know, love and serve God in this world*. And now, in the words of the 'Penny Catechism', they *are happy with him for ever in the next*.

Each one is a proof that Saints are *made*, not *born*. They had the same supernatural means which we have: the Holy Sacrifice of the Mass, the Sacraments, prayer. They took their Christian vocation seriously, as all the baptized are called to do, striving to practise the virtues heroically, relying on God's grace.

Their love for God was always inseparably united to a burning love and zeal for souls – no one can become a saint if concerned only about his or her own salvation. They were effective instruments in drawing others close to God and helping them both humanly and supernaturally, precisely because of their union with him. This was the cause of their peace and happiness, qualities which made each an attractive personality, and enabled them to bring hope and strength to others. Reading the life of a saint has brought many a person closer to God.

The Saints are as varied as the members of the human race, but certain characteristics can be discovered in the lives of all. They spent some time each day in prayer. The Mass was of paramount importance to them. They frequented the Sacraments of Reconciliation and the Holy Eucharist. They had a tender devotion to the Mother of God, and an unswerving loyalty to the Magisterium of the Church, particularly to the Roman Pontiff.

All the Saints were eminently well balanced, with a true order of priorities, giving the first place to God, before turning their attention to other people. They regarded the events of this life with a view to eternity and so were able to keep things in their proper perspective. For them, as He is for us, God was a loving Father who always works or permits what is best for his children.

In some of the Saints we may find a model for our own life, whilst not in others. But in each we can find an intercessor in heaven. We can turn to any of the saints in heaven seeking their prayers and assistance, for our own needs, for those of our fellow-men on earth and for our companions who are still undergoing the purifying sufferings of Purgatory. Through their intercession may we too learn to sanctify this everyday life on earth so that when the time comes we will also deserve to hear the greeting of Our Lord, *'Well done, good and faithful servant, enter into the joy of your Lord.'*

P.K.
22 June 1992

Saint Boniface

ENGLISH APOSTLE OF GERMANY

During the so-called Dark Ages, around 672, a little boy was born into a Christian family and baptised Wynfrith; he is the saint who is better known as Boniface. Their home was Crediton in Devon in the kingdom of Wessex. The conversion of this part of England had been one of the more recent fruits of the labours of Saint Augustine of Canterbury and his monks, who had arrived in the country some seventy years previously. Like most fond parents, Wynfrith's father was planning a secure future for his son; but his plans were upset one day when some travelling monks called at their home. The boy was greatly moved at meeting them, and told his father that he too wished to be a monk. At first his father raised many objections, but being a good Christian at heart he yielded and allowed Boniface to go when he was thirteen to the monastery of Escancester (Exeter) to continue his education. There Boniface's desire was fulfilled and he made his religious profession.

Later, his parents must have thanked God for the wonderful apostolic work carried out by their son, realising then how worthwhile their own sacrifice had been, and what a privilege his vocation had turned out to be for them. Due to Boniface's faithfulness, and thanks to the Christian upbringing he had received in the bosom of his own family, literally thousands of pagans in the lands we know today as Germany and Holland were converted to Christianity. Not so many years ago, Catholic parents used to pray for a vocation for at least one of their children; this could perhaps again be a way of helping towards the re-Christianisation of the Europe in which Saint Boniface was one of the pioneers of Christianity.

Early missionary activity

Boniface was transferred to the monastery of Nhutscelle (Nursling) in the diocese of Winchester, where the Abbot, Winbert, soon employed him to teach a wide range of subjects including rhetoric, poetry, history and Sacred Scripture. He seems to have been an uncommonly enterprising tutor, composing his own textbooks, including a Latin grammar, and writing poetry.

One of the landmarks of his life came at the age of thirty – his ordination to the priesthood by Bishop Daniel of Winchester. To his duties as a teacher he now added those of a pastor, whilst his desires to reach more and more souls continued to grow. By 716 Abbot Winbert gave him permission to travel to Frisia (Holland) to join another Englishman, Saint Willibrord, who had been working there for some twenty years. Full of hope, Saint Boniface and three companions set off from the port of London, only to receive a set-back on arrival in the Low Countries. The pagan duke Radbod was at war with Charles Martel, the Frankish leader, and had taken control of the region, destroying most of the churches in Frisia. Saint Willibrord, the bishop, was in exile and chaos reigned everywhere. Boniface made his way as far as Utrecht, and from there, deciding that he could achieve little or nothing, returned to England and his monastery at Nursling.

Abbot Winbert died shortly after Boniface's return, and he was greatly disconcerted when the other monks unanimously decided to elect him as their new abbot. He pleaded with Bishop Daniel to nominate someone else in his place. The Bishop agreed. He then gave Boniface a letter of recommendation to the Pope, Gregory III, and his blessing for the journey to Rome in 718.

Pope Gregory received him, and having satisfied himself as to his orthodoxy, encouraged Boniface in his apostolic plans, giving him authority to preach to pagans anywhere he found them. The scope of his apostolate was unlimited: Boniface (who was given his new name by this Pope) headed for Germany armed with his papal approval and letters of recommendation from his Holiness to all the Christian rulers whose lands he would visit, asking them to furnish whatever help they could. The journey took Boniface through Bavaria to Thuringia in south-east Germany, where the Irish monk Saint Kilian had preached some time earlier. The Faith, however, had not been deeply rooted, and Boniface discovered to his dismay that priests and people alike had slipped back into their pagan ways. He set to with a will, and eventually obtained the re-conversion of many who had been Christian, and brought great numbers of pagans into the Church for the first time.

News then reached him that Radbod, the pagan ruler of Frisia, had died, and that the Christian Charles Martel had annexed the territory. This for Boniface was an opportunity not to be missed. He made the journey to Frisia to join Saint Willibrord, working with him for the next three years. Together they were instrumental in bringing about innumerable conversions. As Saint Willibrord was getting old he determined to ordain Boniface as bishop to succeed him in the see of Utrecht. Boniface felt that this would greatly limit his scope as a missionary; he needed to be free from any such ties in order to carry out the Pope's mandate and travel to other pagan territories. Saint Willibrord reluctantly agreed, and Boniface set off once more to Hesse, a part of Saxony. Two of his first converts were chieftains whose influence greatly helped his apostolic efforts. There were literally thousands of converts, and with the assistance of their chief men, Boniface built several churches, founded monasteries and set up a centre for the training of native priests. Wherever he went Boniface always ensured the stability and continuity of his work by establishing monasteries, churches and convents. In this way his converts would receive continual instruction and formation in their Faith, thereby avoiding the danger of their falling away.

The German mission

As the Pope had instructed Boniface to consult him about any problems and keep him informed of his work, Boniface sent one of his monks to Rome with a letter explaining what was being done. Pope Gregory sent a reply with his apostolic blessing and an invitation to come to Rome. Boniface started out immediately, reaching Rome in 722. On the 30th of November, Saint Andrew's day, the Pope ordained him Bishop for all Germany. As yet another way of demonstrating his love for the Pope, Boniface before returning to Germany took an ancient oath of loyalty to the Holy See used at that time by the bishops of Italy.

Pope Gregory had worked with him for some time on plans for his future apostolate; he knew the main problems Boniface would be encountering in the German lands, for reports of the situation of the Church there had reached him. In the particular district of Hesse there were very few Christians and very many pagans; Thuringia unfortunately held an unsatisfactory mixture of the two, and the Frisians were permanently at war with the Franks – not an encouraging panorama, but Boniface once again left Rome with even greater zeal. Having the fulness of Holy Orders he could now ordain priests, an enormous step forward in his work as Pastor of so many souls. Part of his 'equipment' was a letter from the Pope for Charles Martel, the powerful ruler of the Franks. Martel was a Christian by faith and a soldier by profession. He it was who finally halted the advance of Islam in Europe by a great victory at Poitiers in 732. By that time Mohammed's followers had conquered Christian North Africa, nearly all of Spain and parts of France including Provence and Burgundy. Charles Martel proved himself invaluable to Boniface's work by affording him protection from the belligerent pagans. None of them dared attack the Christians whilst the Frankish ruler was their guardian. In one of his letters to Bishop Daniel in Winchester Boniface comments: *Without the protection of the King of the Franks I can neither rule the lay-folk of the Church nor defend the priests and clergy, the monks and nuns of God; nor can I avail aught to check heathen rites and the worship of idols in Germany without his mandate and the wholesome fear of him.* (The 'help' of Charles Martel was in actuality something of a mixed blessing, as he had the disconcerting habit of using Church property to reward his commanders and their lieutenants.)

Boniface's first field of apostolate this time was the great province of Hesse. Following the advice received from Bishop Daniel, his usual approach to the pagans was to start with their leaders. He wore his Bishop's robes, carrying a copy of the Gospels, with a silver cross or banner going before him. Rather than directly attacking the heathen gods, he sowed doubt in the minds of their devotees by asking how these 'deities', who had all the limitations of other creatures and had come into existence in the course of time, could have created everything that exists. From there he proceeded to an explanation of the Creed. And all this was in the language of the people.

The Great Tree at Hesse

When occasion required Boniface was quite prepared to use stronger tactics. The people of Hesse worshipped some of the Norse gods, *Thor* and *Woden*, for instance, (who have given us the names of two of the days of the week), and *Saxnote*. The cult of these gods was closely linked to aspects of nature, especially sacred trees. One such tree, an enormous oak, dedicated to Thor, the god of war, stood on a mountain at Geismar, in Hesse. This tree was held to be of mystic significance and had great influence over the people; it was for them the presence of Thor among them. Boniface realised that whilst the tree remained standing, he would make very little progress in his preaching. Being a decisive man he decided to remove it, and, wielding an axe, set to with a will. The people came from far and wide to watch the spectacle, confidently awaiting Thor's vengeance. Boniface calmly continued to chop; the great tree collapsed, and with it the people's belief in Thor. At the same time they conceived a great respect for the God of the Christians and his representative, which paved the way for many conversions. Boniface's finishing touch was to use the wood of the great oak to build a chapel dedicated to Saint Peter – a lesson for all of them (and for us) in devotion to the See of Rome, and banishing forever all connection with Thor and his pantheon.

Enlisting help from other lands

Christianity continued to flourish. Boniface set up the monastery of Saint Michael at Amoeneburg before moving on to Thuringia, where he was to spend the next ten years. There he founded several monasteries which would be permanent centres of prayer, work and education. The task was rapidly outgrowing his resources, so Boniface wrote many letters home to his friends, with whom he had maintained contact throughout the years he had spent abroad. He also wrote a circular letter to all the clergy, religious and lay faithful of England asking for prayers and assistance. The response was extremely generous, both financially and in terms of gifted vestments, sacred vessels, books and all that was necessary to set up churches. By far the most valuable help, however, was the number of volunteers who made the hazardous journey to join him, ready to dedicate themselves wholeheartedly to the work that lay ahead. Catholic Britain took upon itself the responsibility for spreading the Faith to other lands.

The names of some of Boniface's companions have come down to us; it is an impressive list, as the majority are recognised as canonised Saints. One was Saint Lioba, Boniface's cousin, who played an important part in setting up convents in Germany. Shortly before Boniface's death he asked her to remain there for the rest of her life, which she did, staying at her post for many years during which she became a close friend of Hildegard, the wife of Charlemagne and mother of Louis the Pious. Others are Saint Thecla, a relative of Saint Lioba, Saints Willibald and Wynnebald, who were brothers, and their sister Saint Walburge. Boniface always worked as a member of a team; none of them acted as an isolated individual; all had the desire to be humble and effective instruments of God closely united to the Vicar of Christ. The influence of Boniface on these companions of his is just as amazing as the wonderful work he did among the pagans. He led them to take their Faith seriously and give their whole lives to it.

His letters are full of apostolic content. Referring to the duties of pastors, he wrote to Saint Cuthbert, Archbishop of Canterbury: *Let us fight for the Lord in these days of bitterness and affliction. If this be the will of God, let us die for the holy laws of our fathers, that we may arrive with them at the eternal inheritance. Let us not be dumb dogs, sleeping sentinels, that fly at the sight of the wolf; but watchful and diligent pastors, preaching to the great and the small, to the rich and the poor, to every age and condition, being instant in season and out of season.* His homilies make frequent mention of the sanctity and obligation of the baptismal vows. Another attractive side of Boniface's is shown in his letter to a bishop friend, sending his greeting and *two measures of wine*, so that the bishop could enjoy it with his friends. Boniface himself did not drink, and abstinence from alcohol was the rule in his monasteries, but he made no attempt to impose his mortifications on others.

Unity with Peter

In 731 Pope Gregory III succeeded the other Gregory, so Boniface wrote to renew his promise of fidelity and ask the advice of the new Pope concerning some of the problems that had arisen, thus ensuring complete unity with the Church and her visible Head. Boniface himself said on one occasion, *Whatever joy or sorrow came to me, I used to inform the apostolic Pontiff of it so that in joyful things we might praise God together, and so that in sorrowful things I might be strengthened by his counsel, admonition and authority.* Pope Gregory wrote back to Boniface, sending him the pallium making him Archbishop of Germany, with power to set up new bishoprics whilst having no fixed See himself, in order to have freedom of movement for supervision. Boniface began the work of re-organisation, and in 737 travelled for the last time to Rome. The Pope created him his papal legate and instructed him to hold synods twice every year. On Boniface's return he established bishoprics at Salzburg, Freising, Ratisbon and Passau, thus ensuring the continuity of the Church in those parts. Some years later Boniface lost some of his closest friends and helpers; Saint Willibrord died in 739, Pope Gregory III and Charles Martel in 741. The new Pope, Zachary, like his predecessors, recognised the value of Boniface's endeavours and entrusted him with yet another difficult task – the reformation of the Frankish Church, which had fallen into a state of decay. There had been a lack of real organisation for some seventy years, and many ecclesiastical posts were held by thoroughly unworthy individuals. Fortunately the two sons of Charles Martel, Carloman, who ruled in the north, which included Bavaria, and Pepin in the South, including France, were both supporters of Boniface's reforms. The effect of his friendship with Carloman could seem surprising, he being a person of great power and very extensive possessions. But Carloman ruled only for a short while, then deciding to follow Boniface's example. Leaving his lands to Pepin, his younger brother, he went to Rome, and thence to Monte Cassino to become a Benedictine. Boniface clearly did not limit his apostolate to converting pagans. Pepin assumed the royal title of King, and requested Boniface to carry out a solemn coronation ceremony at

Soissons. In fact the ceremony used in Westminster Abbey for the coronation of monarchs in Great Britain derives from this event.

Confirming the faith in the newly converted

As part of his plan of re-organisation and reform Boniface called several important synods, the decisions of which were confirmed by the Holy See. One of these, held at Leptines (Leessines) in 743, fixed the use of the Roman Ritual for the administration of the Sacraments and other liturgical acts – another link strengthening the connection with Rome. There is an interesting addendum to what had been the usual formula of renunciation of the devil in the Baptismal rite. For the benefit of his Saxon converts, Boniface wanted to make it quite clear to them who and what they were renouncing. They added: *End ac forsacho allum diaboles uuercum and uuordum Thunaer ende Woden ende Saxnote end allum them unholdum the hira genotas sint – and I forsake (renounce) all the devil's works and words, Thor and Woden and Saxnote, and all the monsters that are their associates ...*

Boniface always gave great importance to consolidating the faith of his converts, mainly through the subsequent founding of convents and monasteries. One foundation very dear to his heart was the monastery of Fulda founded in 744 by his disciple Saint Sturm. The land for the monastery, in the forest of Buchenau between Hesse and Bavaria, had been a gift from Carloman. The monks were trained by Saint Boniface himself, and he sent Saint Sturm to Monte Cassino for a year to gain experience of Benedictine life in that famous monastery. He appointed Sturm as its Abbot on his return to Fulda. It became a thriving centre of monastic life and pastoral care, and of formation for priests – so essential for the Church. During Saint Sturm's lifetime it came to have over four hundred monks. Boniface spent some time there every year, and did retreats. He expressed a wish to be buried there.

Epilogue

When he was about eighty, Boniface made use of the privilege granted by Pope Zachary and appointed Saint Lullus his successor as Archbishop of Mainz. He did not however go into peaceful retirement – instead he set off once more for Frisia in 754, the country where his apostolic labours had begun. He took with him Bishop Eoban to be the new bishop of Utrecht, and several priests and monks. Their work was very fruitful, and on the 5th of June they went to Dokkum on the river Borne for the Confirmation of a group of recent converts. It was the eve of Pentecost. Suddenly a mob of hostile pagans attacked, killing Saint Boniface and all the Christians assembled there, fifty-two of them in all. It is said that when he was attacked Saint Boniface raised the book he was holding to protect his head. The sword that slew him left its slash-mark on the book, which is now preserved in the abbey of Fulda.

Saint Boniface's body was first taken to Utrecht, then to Mainz, but finally he was taken home and laid to rest in Fulda, the monastery he loved so much. When news of his martyrdom reached England a council of bishops was held. The decision was taken to celebrate his anniversary with the same solemnity as the feast of Saint Augustine of Canterbury and Saint Gregory the Great. The Archbishop of Canterbury, Saint Cuthbert, informed Saint Lullus in Mainz of this, and renewed the arrangement for Masses and prayers between England and Germany – a custom started by Boniface, himself a man whose incredible apostolic work was based constantly on prayer, the Holy Sacrifice of the Mass and unswerving loyalty to Rome.

SAINT CATHERINE OF SIENA

The century into which Catherine Benincasa was born was one of turmoil within the Church and throughout Europe. Cities were devastated by the plague; France and England were engaged in the Hundred Years' War; many of the Italian cities were constantly fighting each other. For seventy years the Popes had been residing at Avignon; their return to Rome was rapidly followed by the Schism of the West.

Catherine, born on the 25th of March 1347, was the twenty-fourth of the twenty-five children of Jacopo Benincasa, dyer, and Monna Lapa, his wife. The couple were well known for their generosity; always ready to help those in need, they even adopted another child, ten-year old Tommaso della Fonte, who had been left an orphan by the plague! When Tommaso was older they enabled him to continue his studies and eventually he became a Dominican priest.

The first call

As a child, Catherine was very high-spirited until a complete change came over her when she was six years old. One day, as she was walking home with her brother Stefano, after visiting their married sister Bonaventura, Catherine suddenly stopped in her tracks. She saw a vision of Our Lord smiling at her and blessing her. Stefano, who had seen nothing, could not understand why his little sister stood rooted to the spot. He pulled her along back to the house, and from then on all the girl desired was to be left alone to think ... and to pray.

Monna Lapa, a very practical woman, assumed that her daughter was sickening for something and thought the best cure would be to keep her busy constantly, running errands and helping in the house. Sometimes Catherine made the excuse of wanting to visit Bonaventura as a means of obtaining a little peace and quiet. This came to an end when she was twelve, as at that time no young girl of that age or upwards would ever go out unchaperoned.

Soon her mother began to make plans for arranging her marriage. Catherine showed no interest in the idea and when an eligible young man was suggested as her future husband, she flatly refused. Her parents insisted; Catherine was adamant – she was not going to get married. At last the priest was called in to see if he could convince the girl to change her mind. He tried, unsuccessfully, and, on leaving the house, suggested half-jokingly, that if she didn't want to get married, she might as well cut off her long hair. No sooner said than done. Off it came. Her parents, understandably, were furious – with the priest first of all but especially with their daughter.

Another plan of attack was tried. Catherine was deprived of her room and made to take the place of the servant in the house. To their amazement and annoyance, the girl accepted quietly and willingly whatever work was demanded of her; she even had an unusual aura of peace about her. Eventually her father decided that enough was enough; Catherine was made one of the family again and given back her own room. Monna Lapa, by now convinced that her Catherine really was ill, hardly allowed her out of her sight, even sleeping in her room as she realized Catherine tended to stay up to pray. She then thought that a course of treatment at the nearby thermal springs might be the answer. Catherine asked her permission to bathe alone. The water bubbled from the source almost at boiling point. Thinking of the terrible pain suffered by the souls in Purgatory, Catherine went into the water as close as possible to the unbearably hot source and offered the pain it caused her for the Holy Souls. Soon after their return home, Catherine became really ill – with smallpox. Poor Monna Lapa was distraught. When her daughter asked her permission to join the Third Order of Saint Dominic she had not the heart to refuse and contacted the Prioress. When Catherine was well again, Monna Lapa went with her for the ceremony in which she received the white dress and black cloak of the Tertiaries in 1364. Catherine was now seventeen.

Since she had been a child, when Our Lord made her see that He had a special mission for her, Catherine had practised prayer and penance. Now she began to increase her mortifications, reducing her food to a minimum – a few spoonfuls a day, sleeping for only two hours at night, and that on a plank. She kept complete silence, apart from Confession, and never left her room except to go to the Church. The other members of the Third Order could not understand why this newcomer made herself so *different*.

Criticism increased when her ecstasy after Holy Communion began to be noticed. For hours after receiving the Sacred Host, she would remain motionless, totally oblivious to all that went on around her – even when someone pierced her feet with a long slender blade to see if she would react. God was all in all to her. Three years of her life of solitude passed by, when Our Lord again appeared to her, accompanied by his mother, surrounded by angels and saints. He made Catherine his mystical spouse, placing a ring on her finger, promising that nothing would ever decrease her faith, as He would be her constant support. Jesus then asked her to fulfil everything He would ask of her. The first demand was that she should give up her isolated way of life, which she loved so much. Catherine obeyed immediately, although it cost her dear to do so.

She calmly proceeded to look after all the domestic duties in the busy household, and started to visit the local hospitals, even the one which was solely for those suffering from the dread disease of leprosy. There, one old woman named Tecca, of whom Catherine took great care – no-one else wanted to – repaid her kindness by spreading horrible calumnies about her. Catherine kept silent and continued to look after Tecca. Very soon, signs of the leprosy showed on her own hands, which she prudently kept hidden from her mother. After some time Tecca died, fully repentant for the evil she had done to her benefactress. Catherine prepared the body and buried it with as much love as she had shown the old lady during her life. When she glanced down at her hands there was no trace of leprosy on them.

In 1374 another epidemic of the plague struck Siena. Catherine spent her days and nights assisting the sick and dying, burying the corpses others refused to touch. Very often, through fear of contagion, the poor sufferers were left alone in their last hours. Catherine ensured that she stayed till the end with as many as she could, comforting them and preparing them for the moment of their judgement. Countless numbers of children died, among them several of her small nephews and nieces.

Guide and peace-maker
Through this work in the hospitals and with the plague victims, many of those in contact with her began

to realize that Catherine had a special gift for understanding and guiding souls. Her advice was sought from all quarters; she never refused anyone who appealed for her aid, whether in person or by letter. Never having attended school, she could neither read nor write, so one of her followers, a Tertiary like herself, Alessa Saracini, acted as her secretary, taking down the replies dictated by Catherine. This was the beginning of a voluminous correspondence, all the letters being examples of the depth of her union with God, supernatural outlook and womanly common sense.

Using the gift she had for reaching peoples' hearts, she acted as peace-maker to settle minor and major quarrels and feuds, travelling to various cities whenever she was asked. By special request of Pope Gregory XI she did all she could to promote his plan for a Crusade to liberate the Holy Places. Wherever she went her very presence attracted crowds, many of whom were instantly won over by her almost tangible holiness, changing their attitudes and their whole lives. Three priests were appointed to join her on her journeys, to hear the confessions of the many penitents who had come to her.

In 1375 her arrival in Pisa was the occasion of a religious revival in that city. She gave herself unstintingly, disregarding her fragile constitution. One morning, during her thanksgiving after Mass in the church of Santa Cristina, the priest noticed her looking up at the Crucifix. Suddenly she collapsed and remained immobile. The priest and her companions hurried over to help her. He heard her say, almost inaudibly, that she had received the marks of the five wounds of Christ on her body; the pain they caused made her think she was about to die. As she fell she had cried out, *Ah, Lord, let these marks be hidden*. They were, during her lifetime, although she felt the pain, and at her death they became visible once more.

When she returned to Siena her remarkable influence over souls became apparent yet again. Niccolo de Toldo, a young nobleman from Perugia, had been sentenced to death for speaking scathingly of the Siena government. The two cities had been on unfriendly terms for some time; appeals for mitigation of the sentence went unheeded. Niccolo rebelled furiously against his fate. In his rage and despair he savagely rejected the attempts of any priests to speak to him and help him to prepare for the next life. The authorities had at least sufficient concern to ask Catherine to try to do something for him. Catherine went to visit the condemned man. Her words and her presence brought about an amazing change. Niccolo went to confession and prepared himself for death. He then asked Catherine to promise to accompany him to the scaffold.

Very early the next morning Catherine took him to Mass and he received Holy Communion for the last time. As she led him back to the cell Catherine said, *Be comforted, my dearest brother, for soon we shall come to the nuptials. You shall go there bathed in the Blood of the Son of God, in the sweet name of Jesus, which I never wish to leave your memory.* Catherine notes that, *his heart then lost all fear and his face was transformed from sadness to joy; he rejoiced, exulted and said, Whence comes so much grace to me that the delight of my soul will await me at the holy place of execution? You see what light he had received when he called the place of execution holy!* Catherine was ready, waiting for him, praying that he would die with peace, and that she might receive the grace of seeing him go to God. She continues, *Then I saw God-and-Man, as one sees the clarity of the sun, receiving that soul in the fire of his divine charity. Oh, how ineffably beautiful it was to see the goodness of God! With what gentleness and love He waited for that soul as it left the body... But Niccolo did a gracious act that would draw a thousand hearts... He turned back like a spouse who has reached the threshold of her new home, who looks round and bows to those who accompanied her, showing her gratitude by that ges- ture.* So died one of the innumerable souls for whom Catherine won the grace of repentance and perfect love of God.

Love for the Church

More than the majority of her contemporaries, Catherine was intensely aware of the pressing needs of the time. For her the first was the reform of the Church, for which she had an extraordinarily deep and tender love. She saw that the first step was for the Popes to leave Avignon and return to the See of Peter. Peace between the warring factions in Italy was also a priority, and the great Crusade to liberate the Holy Land and bring the faith of Christ to the Muslims. The Crusade would be the means of uniting the Italian cities and other Christian nations to fight for a common cause, but the return of the Pope to Rome came before all else. Since 1309 when Clement V had left the eternal city for Avignon, the prestige of the papacy had declined throughout Christendom. Many suspected, not without foundation, that the Popes were yielding to pressure from France. By Catherine's time most of the Cardinals were French. They elected French Popes. They had no wish to return to Rome, which had endured much from the constant battles between lead- ing families and the invasions of mercenary troops. The papal court at Avignon was worldly, filled with clerics who, though efficient administrators, were not outstanding for their virtues. As a result, clerical discipline grew lax, the people were without guidance from their pastors, the Christian princes were constantly at war with each other. Saint Bridget of Sweden had for years repeated her warnings of what would befall the Church unless the Popes went back to Rome. In 1367 Pope Urban V did go. He entered Rome amid great rejoicing, but his stay was short. He became ill because of the climate and after three years went back again to Avignon, dying there a few months later. The Cardinals then elected another French Pope – Gregory XI. He announced his intention of going to Rome, but by 1376 had still not taken a firm decision to do so. Catherine sent letters to Gregory exhorting him to have courage and do what he knew was right for the Church. She then went to Avignon to speak to him personally. Finally she prevailed. Pope Gregory XI entered Rome in 1377, bitterly opposed by the Cardinals.

By this time Catherine had a large following of disciples, Tertiaries like herself (one of whom was her mother, a widow now), religious from various Orders and laymen. Several had undergone a profound conversion due to their contact with her, and despite the fact that Catherine was much younger than most of them – she was still in her twenties – they called her *Mamma* and followed her guidance faithfully. Through her help many made great progress in their interior life. She continued to journey from one city to another with her companions, pacifying feuding families and cities. Whilst in Florence in April 1378 negotiating for peace between the cities forming the Tuscan League, headed by Florence itself, and the papal armies, news came that Gregory XI had died. Trouble began as soon as the Cardinals prepared for the conclave to elect a successor. The Vatican was mobbed by crowds in the streets shouting *We want a Roman!* The conclave was very short, and the candidate chosen, though not Roman, was an Italian, the Archbishop of Bari, who took the name Urban VI.

The new Pope was keen to effect far-reaching reforms in the Church, but his intolerance and tactless manner alienated the Cardinals, who soon regretted their choice. Catherine, aware of the urgency of the need for reform, also saw that this had to be undertaken with a more diplomatic approach. In her first letter to the Pontiff she had the courage to remind him respectfully that *Justice without mercy is clouded with cruelty*. One of Catherine's disciples, in an audience with Urban VI was also the recipient of an outburst of anger. He remained respectful and silent ... but Catherine realized only too well that the Cardinals would not be so submissive. Very soon the Cardinals took matters into their own hands. They went to Anagni and there declared the Holy See to be vacant, insisting that they had only elected Urban out of fear of the mob. The French cardinals were then joined by the Italians, who had hesitated at first. The group then proceeded to Fondi, to be under the protection of the Count, who was at enmity with Urban. Their intention was to hold a conclave.

Catherine sent a letter with all haste to the Count, begging him not to act as protector to the Cardinals, and reminding him that Urban was truly the Pope. In her letter to the Cardinals she did not mince her words. She told them that they knew very well the election had been valid; they were all cowards, acting as instruments of the devil. She also sent a letter to the Pope, by then deserted by the whole college of Cardinals, to encourage him. All her efforts were of no avail. The conclave was held and a rival *'Pope'* chosen, Robert of

Geneva, who took the name of Clement VII. The great Western Schism had taken place. In her love for the Church, Catherine was heart-broken; she strove even more to make people react, sending letters to the Catholic rulers of Europe, the cardinals and bishops, pleading with them to be loyal to Urban. The latter did not help her task because of his intransigence. Catherine besought him to be prudent and to forgive those who acknowledged their errors, but he refused.

Open war then broke out between the armies of the Pope and the anti-Pope. Catherine knew that soon she would have to go to Rome to help Urban, who eventually summoned her. Before leaving Siena she dictated her *Dialogue of Divine Providence* – a conversation between her soul and God. It covers the entire plan of the Redemption, recording her ecstasies, showing her amazing penetration into the mysteries of faith. She stresses the fact that love for God and for one's neighbour are inseparable – the soul who truly loves God loves and serves others of necessity. She speaks ardently of her love for the Church, for the Roman Pontiff, *the Christ in the world who holds the keys of the Blood of the humble Lamb*. Addressing the Pope she calls him *the sweet Christ on earth*, and on reaching Rome she again offered her life for the Church.

She prayed and fasted as never before. More and more letters were sent to civil and ecclesiastical authorities imploring them to support Pope Urban. In Saint Peter's basilica, praying before a mosaic of Peter's boat tossed by the storm, she had a vision in which she felt the whole weight of the boat – the Church – pressing unbearably upon her. She collapsed to the floor and when her friends carried her back to where she was staying they found that she was partially paralysed. She was no longer able to leave her room; Mass was celebrated there daily. Unable to eat or drink, Catherine lived literally on her daily reception of the Holy Eucharist.

On Sunday, the 29th of April 1380, she died surrounded by Monna Lapa, her elderly mother, and a group of her followers. She was just thirty-three years old. Her body, clothed in the black and white Dominican habit, was laid by her companions in the church of Santa María sopra Minerva. As soon as news of her death reached the people of Rome they flocked to the church to honour her. She was considered by many to be a saint. Some brought their sick relatives and friends to be near her — miraculous cures took place, and devotion to her spread swiftly in Italy and abroad. The young woman who spent her life serving the Church with all her might continued this work even more fruitfully after her death.

She was canonized by another Sienese – Pope Pius II – in 1461. Pius IX in 1886 proclaimed her as second patron saint of Rome, and in 1939 Pius XII named her with Saint Francis of Assisi as primary patrons of Italy. More recently Pope Paul VI gave her, with Saint Teresa of Avila, the title of Doctor of the Church, as a tribute to the value of her mystical and ascetical teaching, which has guided countless souls in their search for the Way, the Truth and the Life.

Saint Charles Borromeo

Saint Charles Borromeo was born, the second of six children, on the 2nd of October, 1538. His father, Gilberto Borromeo, was Count of Arona; his mother, Margharita, was the sister of Giovanni Angeli de'Medici, the future Pope Pius IV. The early years of Charles' life were spent in the castle of Arona, close to beautiful Lake Maggiore, and in the Palazzo Borromeo in Milan, where he attended school before going to the university of Pavia to study civil and canon law. Although the family were very wealthy, his father did not allow his young son to have much money at his disposal, which helped Charles later to be detached from the material goods with which he was surrounded, and to have a great love for the poor. His father died in 1558, and even though he was not the eldest son, the family sent for him to arrange their affairs, after which he resumed his studies, obtaining his doctorate when only twenty-two years old, and returned to Milan.

Life in Rome

News reached the family in 1559 that Cardinal de'Medici (Charles' maternal uncle) had been elected Pope on the 26th of December, taking the name of Pius IV. The new Pope, who had always had great affection for his nephew and high esteem for his qualities, sent for him in 1560. From then on Charles' life was changed completely. He was created Cardinal deacon at the unusual age of twenty-three, and was given a number of important tasks – those of being Administrator of the Archdiocese of Milan; Delegate of Bologna, Romagna and Ancona; Protector of the Kingdom of Portugal, Lower Germany and the Catholic Swiss cantons; as well as Protector of several religious orders – all of which he took on with a great sense of responsibility. Somehow, in spite of all the work, he still managed to find time to study and have profitable leisure – he played the lute and the violin, and was proficient at a ball game typical of the time.

Working so close to the Holy Father, Saint Charles soon learned what a heavy burden lay upon the shoulders of the Pontiff. The effects of the so-called Reformation had devastated the Church throughout Europe, the errors of Luther, Calvin and Zwingli spreading like wildfire. The English king Henry VIII, by declaring himself head of the Church, had caused a whole nation to be separated from Rome. There were cruel persecutions and many martyrs. Doctrinal confusion was rife.

The Council of Trent

This great Council, which counteracted the innumerable protestant errors, stating in precise formulas the perennial teachings of the Church, was begun by Pope Paul III in 1545. The course of the Council had been interrupted several times, mainly due to interference on the part of the Emperor, Philip II of Spain and of Henry III of France, for plainly political reasons. One such break in the Council lasted from 1552 until 1562, when Saint Charles was instrumental in having all the members re-assemble. As the Pope's health was poor, Charles felt that it was urgent for the Council to be brought to a conclusion as soon as possible. The closing session was held in 1563, and in it all the decrees of the previous sessions were confirmed. It is thanks to this Council that we have the definitions concerning, among other weighty matters, the sources of Revelation, original sin, grace, the Sacraments, Purgatory, prayer to the saints and indulgences. Charles had spent several years working with his uncle Pius IV in the Council; then came the formidable task of transmitting to the whole Church all the doctrine and the vital measures for improving Christian life.

Saint Charles' choice

Shortly before the end of the Council in 1562 news came that Federico, Charles' elder brother and heir to the family estates, had died. As so much was at stake, his relatives urged Charles to leave the clerical state (he was a deacon), and marry, and thus continue to manage their affairs. Saint Charles chose at this moment to give up all involvement in material concerns and dedicate his life entirely to God by being ordained priest. This ordination took place in the Basilica of Saint Mary Major in Rome on the 4th of September 1563. On the 7th of December of the same year he was ordained bishop in the Sistine Chapel.

Saint Charles threw himself wholeheartedly into working on the catechism of the Council for parish priests, the reform of the missal and breviary, and also the reform of Church music. He chose Palestrina to compose three Masses among other means of contributing to the dignity of the liturgy. Involvement in the Council left Charles with a permanent awareness of the need to give clear doctrine to as many souls as possible, from small children to those who were in a position to reach many others – the priests. With the latter in mind, the Pope had requested all the bishops to found a seminary in each diocese to ensure the sound formation of the clergy. Saint Charles founded one in Rome and entrusted it to the Jesuits. The teaching of sound doctrine in these seminaries was guaranteed by a profession of faith in the teachings of the Council, which was to be upheld by all clerics and by those involved in teaching.

Concern for the diocese of Milan

From the time of his being made Administrator of the diocese four years earlier, Saint Charles had always had a great concern for Milan and the other areas belonging to his care. Being unable to go personally because of his duties in the Vatican, he had arranged for others to represent him there, choosing men who were known for their holiness and experience. One of these was Nicholas Ormanetto, who had accompanied Cardinal Pole to England during the reign of Queen Mary. Saint Charles felt the responsibility for his diocese very deeply, and also wondered whether it might be God's will for him to enter a monastery. When the opportunity presented itself, he consulted the holy archbishop Bartholomew of Braga, Portugal, on his *ad limina* visit to Rome, explaining his problems. The Archbishop set his mind at rest, telling him to remain at his post, serving the universal Church, and to go to his own diocese when the time came. Throughout his life Saint Charles always took care to receive spiritual guidance for his soul, something which in recent centuries of the Church's history has tended to be seen as a real necessity only for priests and members of religious orders. Evidently, though, the practice of receiving spiritual direction is beginning to be more widespread among the laity at a time precisely when, following on from the teaching of Vatican II, the universal call to holiness for everybody is being emphasised.

Saint Charles continued to work in the Vatican,

mentioning to the Pope his desire to go to Milan; some time later, the Pope nominated him Legate for Italy, sending him in this capacity to Milan. The Milanese received their Archbishop with heartfelt celebration. He was the first to reside there for eighty years. His first act after the solemn entry into the city was very significant – Saint Charles processed to the Cathedral, where he spent considerable time in prayer before the Blessed Sacrament. He wasted no time in getting down to business. He immediately summoned a provincial council, which was attended by twelve hundred priests, several bishops and two foreign cardinals, who were astonished at the way the Archbishop handled everything. He was, remember, only twenty-six years of age at the time. Saint Charles produced his plans for systematic catechetical instruction in all parishes (he was the founder of the Confraternity for Christian Doctrine), and for reforms in accordance with the decrees of the Council. He opened a seminary and set about visiting his diocese.

Pope Saint Pius V: Reforms in the Church

In the midst of his activity Saint Charles was summoned to Rome, as his uncle Pope Paul was seriously ill. He reached the Vatican in time to assist the Pope during his last days, accompanied by another saint – Philip Neri. The Pope died on the 10th of December 1565. Saint Charles then took part in the conclave which elected Saint Pius V in January 1566. The new Pope, although wishing to keep Saint Charles with him, knew how urgently reform was needed in the Milan diocese, as elsewhere, and allowed him to go back there. When the previous Pope had initiated his programme for reform he had invited the Archbishop of Braga to help with a thorough series of consultations, beginning with the cardinals and in particular with his nephew Charles. The Archbishop had told the Holy Father that if all the cardinals were like Saint Charles, they could be held up as models for the rest of the clergy.

Saint Charles too began his reforms, but made sure to start with himself. He increased his penances, especially in Lent, but without attracting attention to himself. He always followed the advice of his spiritual director, and lived his spirit of mortification very cheerfully. Once when the weather was very cold he found one of his attendants trying to warm his bed. Saint Charles told him, *the best way not to find the bed cold is to go to bed colder than the bed is!* He spent very little on himself, being at the same time very generous with anyone in need, and in looking after everything connected with the liturgy – restoring churches, providing the best possible sacred vessels etc. – a sign of his deep faith in the real presence of Christ in the Blessed Sacrament. He ate sparingly and slept little. Although the particular ways in which Saint Charles practised mortification may not always be appropriate for everyone to imitate, the spirit of it is, and perhaps more so in our more materialistic consumer society which encourages excessive love of comfort and pleasure-seeking, far removed from the 'narrow path' taught by Our Lord. Saint Charles saw his mortifications as a way of uniting himself to the sufferings of Our Lord, making reparation and winning grace for those whom he wanted to help.

The way in which Saint Charles started to put the reforms into effect with his priests was far from being on the purely organisational level – his concern was for their spiritual lives. He prepared a plan similar to that which he himself lived: daily prayer, Holy Mass, spiritual reading, weekly confession, fasting at certain times. He then went on to arrange councils, synods and methods of teaching doctrine. He founded the Oblates of Saint Ambrose, a congregation of secular priests to help in this, entrusting to them churches, schools and the running of the seminary. One doctrine which he stressed was the importance of the vows made by all the faithful at baptism, echoed, indeed, in our own time in the teaching of Vatican II and the *Christifideles laici* of Pope John Paul II.

Opposition

Saint Charles was outstanding for his charity, patience and tact, which enabled him to win over those he was trying to reform. He had dealt with kings, cardinals, and politicians, and had even been asked for advice by the Popes. His work was not, however, all plain sailing. In 1567 he met opposition from the civil authorities, who even went so far as to arrest one of his officials. Charles excommunicated those concerned; they eventually capitulated. The work of the Church in Switzerland was very difficult, due mainly to the influence of the doctrines of Zwingli. By his persevering efforts the Archbishop restored order, judiciously placed several experienced preachers, and won back to the faith many who had been led astray.

Back in Milan, some houses and members of religious orders were reluctant to put the reforms of the Council of Trent into effect, as was the case with two of the Archbishop's aunts who were nuns. They were adamant in their refusal to obey until the Pope himself wrote to their convent, reminding them that the decrees for reform came from the Holy See. One group of clerics, the Humiliati, after their reform wished to return to their previous condition, permission

for which the Archbishop refused. Four of them then
planned to assassinate him. One, disguised as a layman,
entered the Archbishop's chapel with other members
of the public when Saint Charles was kneeling before
the altar preparing to lead the evening prayers. The
intruder shot the Archbishop in the back, escaping in
the ensuing panic. Saint Charles indicated that those
present should continue the prayers, and thinking he
was mortally wounded, commended himself to God. To
the amazement of everyone, the ball had not even
penetrated his vestments, but had caused no more than
a swelling on his back (which remained for the rest of
his life). Saint Charles entreated the public authorities
not to search for his would-be killers, as he forgave
them; but in spite of his efforts to save them they were
arrested and executed. Another group refused him
entry into their church, and again he was fired at, the
cross he was carrying being damaged. When these
assailants saw how Saint Charles had forgiven his other
enemies, they repented, publicly asked for pardon, and
were forgiven also. He was far less concerned about
personal attacks than about all the dangers to the
Church from the various heresies and from the persist-
ing Muslim threat. Saint Charles firmly supported Saint
Pius V in his endeavours to exhort and encourage all
Christians to have recourse to the Rosary as a way of
warding off the danger. Christians responded; they
prayed to Our Lady and the famous battle of Lepanto
was won, freeing Christendom from the peril.

Natural disasters – the heroism of Saint Charles
        The year 1571 brought a very poor harvest in the
area around Milan, causing great hardship. Many were
starving. The Archbishop worked unceasingly to provide aid, supporting around three thousand people

daily from his own means. This help was multiplied, since, when the governor and other dignitaries saw his example, they too gave generous donations. Saint Charles became ill, and was in a weak state when it was announced that Pope Saint Pius V had died. In spite of his condition, Saint Charles made the journey to Rome, to the conclave in which was elected Gregory XIII, the Pope who is known for his Congregation for the Propagation of the Faith. Then in 1576 an epidemic of the dreaded plague broke out in Venice, Mantua and Milan. The Archbishop immediately left Rome for his diocese, prepared himself for death, made his will and gave himself entirely to the care of the sick and dying. Because of his example of heroic charity, a number of priests joined him, knowing that they too were endangering their own lives, but happy to do so for the souls who needed them. Saint Charles organised penitential processions, himself walking barefoot, to make reparation and pray for the end of the epidemic. By the beginning of 1578 it had ceased. In fulfilment of a promise the citizens of Milan built a church which was dedicated to Saint Sebastian, in thanksgiving for their deliverance. The work of reform continued.

The secret of his extraordinary capacity for reaching souls, for carrying out reforms, for setting up so many centres of education, was the saint's life of union with God. Despite pressure of work, he never neglected the time given to prayer, to the Mass and frequent reception of the sacrament of penance. As a preparation for Mass, he tried to be recollected as much as possible from the previous night, and always spent considerable time afterwards in thanksgiving. He prayed often about the Passion of Our Lord, and had a great devotion to Our Lady, making pilgrimages to her shrines at Loretto and Einsiedeln. He made a point of saying vocal prayers with care and attention, and of reading all the prayers of the breviary, even though he knew most of them by heart, as a way of avoiding distractions and routine. He had a deep love of the Cross and carried with him a small relic of the true Cross in a golden reliquary. Whenever possible he would make his prayer near the tabernacle, and struggled to keep an awareness of the presence of God throughout his day. When someone asked him how he might improve his piety, he said, *He who desires to make any progress in the service of God must begin every day of his life with new ardour, must keep himself in the presence of God as much as possible, and must have no other view or end in all his actions but the divine honour.* Each year he made a retreat, and went to confession regularly to the same confessor in order to have effective spiritual guidance. Another of his practices which shows his prudence and love for his priestly celibacy was that of not entering into conversation with a woman unless other persons were present, and of keeping the conversation to what was strictly necessary. He put the needs of others before his own, and whilst being kind and patient had no hesitation in using strong measures when the good of a soul required it.

The end of his life

By 1584 his health had deteriorated to such an extent that to celebrate Holy Mass and keep up with his enormous correspondence had become very difficult. He returned to Milan after a retreat and was given the Viaticum. He died, aged forty-six, whilst the Passion was being read to him, uttering the words, *Ecce venio – Behold, I am coming –* on the 3rd of November. He had spent his whole life joyfully serving the Church and the Pope in a very direct way. In 1610 he was canonized by Pope Paul V, as devotion to him had spread very quickly from Milan, and even to England by the end of the 16th century. He had a portrait of Saint John Fisher, the martyred Bishop of Rochester, for whom he had great veneration, and had spent some time with Saint Edmund Campion, another of the English martyrs, who stayed with him in Milan for a short time on his way to England.

BLESSED DOMINIC BARBERI

WORKING FOR
THE CONVERSION OF ENGLAND

Dominic Barberi, Blessed Dominic of the Mother of God, deserves to be remembered when so much is being done to bring our separated brethren, with whom we share a common Baptism, to a greater understanding of the Catholic Faith, and hopefully, through the grace of God, to complete union and a full acceptance of all the teachings of Jesus Christ. This holy, humble Passionist priest who literally wore himself out through prayer, penance and preaching for the conversion of England was God's instrument in showing many of his contemporaries the path to Rome. Heaven alone knows how many later converts are also indebted to him.

He was born on the 22nd of June 1792 at Pallanzana, near Viterbo, Italy, and was baptised Domenico Giovanni Luigi two days later. His parents, Giuseppe Barberi and María Antonia (née Pacelli), owned a small farm. Dominic, the youngest of their family, was a lively child, gifted with an exceptional memory which was to stand him in good stead in later life. His parents, particularly his mother, taught the children their Faith, instilling into them an especially deep devotion to Our Lady.

Experience of sorrow came at an early age; first Giuseppe, his father, died in 1798, shortly before Dominic's sixth birthday, then a few years later one of his sisters, aged ten, collapsed and died. Five years went by, and then his mother María Antonia died, leaving Dominic feeling desolate. He turned in his grief to Our Lady: *You see that I am deprived of a mother on earth, so now it is up to you to be my Mother!* Our Lady never let him down.

School was not considered an essential part of a farmer's son's life in those times. Dominic was never sent to school. However much some of our youngsters might envy him this protracted *holiday*, Dominic had an insatiable desire to learn to read, to study. He started on his own with a copy of the alphabet, and eventually had a few classes of reading and grammar from some kindly Capuchin monks when they could find the time to take him. On occasion, after walking over a mile to his lesson, he had to return home untaught as the monks had been called to other more urgent duties. But once he had mastered the art of reading, nothing could hold him back. He read whatever he could lay his hands on – much that was good, some that was not. Because of his extraordinary memory he could recite whole pages after one or two readings, a power which he retained when older, being at length able to quote extensively from the Sacred Scriptures in Latin, and to repeat practically verbatim entire sermons he had heard.

The Passionists

After María Antonia's death the property was sold and the children went to live with various relations. Dominic's maternal uncle Bartolomeo Pacelli and his wife Cecilia were delighted to adopt him as their son. They had no children of their own, and treated him with great affection. As with his parents, it never occurred to them to send the boy to school, so without guidance, he read quite indiscriminately until he came up against a crisis of faith. Fortunately he met four Passionist monks who had come to stay as guests of a neighbouring family. By order of Napoleon Bonaparte the religious orders had been suppressed, and the monks and nuns dispersed. Divine Providence made use of this setback to show Dominic his future vocation. The monks allowed him access to their books. One taught him French, but most of all they helped him to grow in interior life, teaching him how to do mental prayer. Dominic felt that God wanted him to be a Passionist, but could see no way of fulfilling this vocation, since officially the Congregation no longer existed. Leaving his problem in God's hands, he thought of one practical thing he could do, which was to teach himself Latin. This he did with a Bible and a Latin dictionary during his spare time. He always attributed his progress to the help of Our Lady; he came to an understanding of the spiritual sense of the Scriptures, *which*, he said, *was not the fruit of my own effort ... because I could never discover it unless God enlightened my mind with a special light.*

When the Pope re-established the Passionists, Dominic immediately asked permission to join the order. By now (1814) he was twenty-two and had not received any formal education. He was admitted after a short delay, and whilst praying before the Lady altar he felt that he was called to work for souls outside the Church, especially in England. In 1818 he was ordained, and wrote a description of this great event in *A Dialogue Between a Young Priest and the Blessed Virgin*. In it he told of his overwhelming joy, his feeling of unworthiness, the gentle reassurances of Our Lady. Imagine, the Blessed Virgin tells him, that you are receiving my Son as I received him in my womb when He was incarnate, or as I welcomed him to my arms when He was born, or as I embraced him on the road to Calvary; or again, as I received him into my arms when they took him down from the Cross ... Offer the Blood of Jesus then, my son, for the conversion of poor sinners and of heretics; remember that they too are my children, redeemed by the Precious Blood of my Divine Son. From then on, Dominic never forgot to pray for the conversion of England, and urged everyone else to do so.

The following was found in his diary: *In this month of October I have experienced a great longing for the conversion of unbelievers, especially in England, and have offered myself to God to be annihilated, if annihilation could serve this purpose. I must make sure that this desire is never extinguished, for I am certain that, if I persevere, God will be moved to pity.* His desire to work in England grew as the years passed; after every class he would lead three Hail Marys for the conversion of this country, and he involved the other Passionists in a campaign of continuous prayer for that same intention. Although the likelihood of his going to England seemed remote, Dominic searched for ways and means to attain his objective – conversions to the Faith in England. His knowledge of the language was minimal, but this did not deter him from teaching the monk who attended the door of the monastery a short speech to be directed towards any British person who happened to call. It started by asking whether or not the person was a Catholic. When the reply was in the negative, the doorkeeper was to proceed: *There is only one God, one true Faith, only one Church founded by Jesus Christ on earth, and that is the Catholic Church.* Then came the main point. *Do you wish to be instructed now that you have the opportunity?* (Dominic was to be called if the visitor showed interest). The reactions of callers must have varied considerably once they had recovered from their surprise and amusement at the rather original pronunciation and idiom. It is said that a Scotsman who was highly entertained and totally unconvinced at the time somehow could not get out of his mind what he had heard. Later he returned to the monastery to inform the monks that he and his friends had all become Catholics ...

Belgium and England

Despite his early lack of education Dominic made up for it during his priestly life. He was chosen as one of the lecturers in theology and preached numerous retreats, while still finding time to write on many themes – catechetical instruction, theological treatises, works on the Passion, on Our Lady, on philosophy... His contemporaries did not always appreciate the depth of his understanding. He was severely rebuked, for example, for his criticism of the works of de Lamennais, who was almost universally acclaimed as a great thinker and writer. Dominic was concerned about the effect that the widespread views of de Lamennais regarding human reason would have when taken to their logical conclusion – cynicism and disbelief. Dominic's penetrating mind had recognised the errors, but he was considered by the intellectuals of his time to be no more than an upstart. He was made to suffer a great deal until in 1833 de Lamennais' errors were condemned by the Holy See. Dominic's worth as a philosopher and theologian was beginning to achieve recognition.

By 1840 he found himself somewhat nearer his objective; he was sent to Belgium to start a monastery there. Ill-health had plagued him for many years; the cold and shortage of food in his new country added to his infirmities, but he accepted it all cheerfully, offering it to God. A campaign of slander was directed against him and the other three monks, which caused them much suffering. Then, to their sorrow, the youngest of them, who had been ill for some time, died. Gradually the sanctity of the three remaining priests began to bear fruit. Dominic was asked to preach in several places and their apostolic work grew. At the end of the same year he received an invitation from Bishop (later Cardinal) Wiseman to visit England. He was beside himself with joy.

His rather romantic hopes were dashed on arrival. It was November the 5th and the traveller, dressed as a secular priest (no religious habits were allowed in public by law), found 'No Popery' signs and effigies of the Pope being burned. Not an auspicious start. Worse was to follow. The house he had been promised, Aston Hall, still had an occupant, who refused to leave; the Passionist could not move in. Gradually Dominic began to understand more about the obstacles they would encounter. After three hundred years of persecution in one way or another, the English Catholics were extremely reticent, and wary of anything that could draw attention to them. Dominic returned to Belgium sadder and wiser. He returned again to England, for good this time, on October the 5th, 1841. Not until February of the following year was he able to go to Aston Hall, the first Passionist house in England. This was not the end of his problems, however. The parishioners expressed their resentment at the *foreigners* in no uncertain terms. His English, or lack of it, provoked unsympathetic laughter. Little by little his hearers were won over rather by what they saw than what they heard. They still had difficulty in understanding him, but his love of God and of souls conveyed its own message. Prejudice among the Catholics was overcome. At first they had been startled and annoyed to see the monks wearing their habits in and around Aston, but now many began to admire them. Children in particular were quick to recognise him as a friend and give him their trust. Nor were they the only ones. Within four months of his arrival he was able to write to a correspondent: *I received four other persons into the bosom of the Church ... now there are seven received.* Soon he had begun instructions for Catholics and any Protestants who were interested, hearing Confessions and celebrating Mass in the village of Stone, where Mass had not been said since the Reformation in the sixteenth century. He visited Stone every Sunday, spending the entire day there, the climax being an evening lecture for non-Catholics only. To everyone's amazement these lectures turned out to be extremely popular; as many as seven hundred at a time crowded in and around to hear him. Both Catholics and Protestants were soon moved to take decisive steps in their interior life. Catholics regained fervour and assisted him in teaching the non-Catholic children whose parents were under Dominic's instruction. A large number of non-Catholics were converted.

This apostolic work did not pass unnoticed, especially among the Protestant clergy, who were indignant at these inroads. Trouble was in store. At first this was purely verbal. The ministers hastened to organise their services so as to have them coincide with his in an endeavour to keep their congregations away from the 'idolatrous Papist'. They even built a new church close to Dominic's. When all this proved ineffectual in stemming the tide of converts, tactics were changed. A gang of young fellows awaited Dominic on his way over to Stone, jeering and throwing a variety of missiles. One

Protestant eye-witness, aged ten at the time, could never forget Dominic's reaction when the first stone found its target. He bent, picked it up, kissed it and put it in his pocket. The boy later became a Catholic, as, it seems, did the gang leader... Dominic persevered with his preaching, although attempts were made to disrupt it from within and without. It took time before his courtesy, serenity and gentleness silenced the opposition, but he suffered much in the interim. Writing to a priest friend he exclaimed: *Last Sunday I broke down and wept bitterly. I can do no more. The cross is too heavy. My God, if you intend to increase the weight of it, you must increase my strength too.*

Soon, because of the increased numbers of Catholics, it was possible to build a church and a school beside it. Then came the longed-for event which gave immense joy to Dominic. He organised a Corpus Christi procession out of doors, the first time for hundreds of years that such a ceremony in honour of the Blessed Sacrament had taken place. Dominic's faith and love for Our Lord knew no bounds, and inevitably attracted other souls. His description of that first procession speaks for itself: *Last Thursday, the feast of Corpus Christi, (1844), we had a beautiful procession in our grounds, with all possible splendour – triumphal arches and altars and a sermon preached out of doors! There were present fully a thousand people, half of whom were Protestants. Yesterday we repeated the ceremony and this time it was even more magnificent. I believe there were over a thousand Protestants there, and just as many Catholics, from all parts. I hope it will not go without fruit. Such things have never been seen in this country before. You could scarcely believe the impression that is made on our own Catholic people, and the enthusiasm excited, as well as the wonderment of the*

Protestants, astounded at their first sight of the magnificence of Catholic worship. At the blessing, everybody knelt, including the Protestants. The following year the procession was held again, this time attended by over five thousand people. On this occasion an unusual occurrence added to the splendour. The procession was scheduled for three o'clock. Rain had been falling steadily since early morning, in such torrents that some of the priests advised Dominic to cancel it. Dominic was not at all perturbed. *Rain will not fall on the Blessed Sacrament*, he said. Everything started at three o'clock on the dot, and the rain continued – except in the church grounds where the procession passed. Protestants as well as Catholics attributed this to a special grace of God in response to Dominic's faith and trust in him. To Dominic, no effort was too great in order to show love and gratitude to Our Lord in the Blessed Sacrament; his example enkindled a similar devotion in others; the way he would make a genuflection or the sign of the Cross was more eloquent than many sermons.

Other devotions

The Rosary was one of Dominic's favourite *weapons* with which to obtain conversions, and in his preaching he often spoke of it, and of the Passion of Our Lord. He often reminded his congregations of the need to receive the Sacraments frequently and well-prepared, and spent hours at a time in the confessional. Saint Joseph was another unfailing support to whom he turned in all his needs, both spiritual and material, and he seems to have obtained special graces on feast days of this Saint.

Parish missions were also re-introduced on Dominic's initiative. The first he was asked to give turned out to be a great ordeal for him. His English was still far from perfect. He did not know the people and he was nervous. Consequently, his audience could hardly understand a word he said. He was bitterly disappointed, and so was the parish priest who had invited him. He struggled on with the evening session, with the same result. Then a man went to see him in the sacristy, asking him to hear his Confession. On being asked what in the sermon had moved him to do so, he said that he had hardly understood anything at all, and did not know what *foreign language* Dominic was speaking. Just the sight of *the holy man* had made him wish to go to confession to him. From then on, things improved; the people became accustomed to his fractured English. His straightforwardness and simplicity, speaking of God's love, touched their hearts. Several non-Catholics were converted as a result of this first mission, which was only the first of very many. He had an attractive way of ensuring that his message went home. This is what he said at the end of one retreat: *During the retreat you have been very fervent and devout, and have been singing in your hearts 'Glory be to the Father and to the Son and to the Holy Spirit'. Let us hope that when the retreat is over, it will not be a case of 'as it was in the beginning, is now and ever shall be!'*

His dealings with others: The Oxford Movement

Despite his poor health, Dominic never spared himself, especially when others needed him, particularly for hearing confessions. Like Saint John Vianney, the Curé d'Ars, he spent hours in the confessional after his mission sermons, during which he always appealed to those present to take the opportunity of making a good confession. Frequently he was still there until the early hours of the morning, never giving the impression of being tired. The greater the number of penitents the happier he was, knowing that souls were restored to friendship with God, with all their sins, however grievous, forgiven.

In his dealings with non-Catholics Dominic was distinguished by his unfailing charity, understanding and, at the same time, clarity in explaining Catholic doctrine. He was very hurt by the attitude of Catholics who were bigoted or abusive in their comments to or about the Protestants. On more than one occasion he put a stop to a series in newspapers of correspondence between Catholics, which had become bitter and prejudiced. This he achieved by writing personally to the parties concerned, tactfully showing them the harm they were doing. In each case they heeded his advice and the acrimonious correspondence ceased. Like Saint Francis de Sales he was of the opinion that one catches more flies with a spoonful of honey than with a barrel-full of vinegar. His attitude is exemplified in his letters to the Anglicans of Oxford University, eminent lecturers and tutors, clergymen who were seeking the unification of the Church of England with Rome; they were taking the approach that the thirty-nine articles of Anglicanism could be accepted in a Catholic sense. These men, including John Henry Newman, John Dobree Dalgairns, Pusey and Keble, produced a series of 'Tracts' concerning doctrinal matters, explaining the Anglican point of view. Dominic sent a reply, in Latin, expressed clearly and logically, but in such a kindly way that the recipients did not feel offended. This gave rise to a series of letters, the correspondence carried out in Latin, with Dominic answering queries and objections and explaining the nature of the Catholic Church.

One stumbling-block for the Tractarians was, as they saw it, a lack of sanctity in the Catholic Church in

England. As Dalgairns put it, let there be found amongst them a saint like the seraph of Assisi. Newman wrote to his friend: *That we must change too, I do not deny. Rome must change first of all in her spirit. We must see more sanctity in her than we do at present.* A rather sad reflection on his Catholic contemporaries.

In 1844 Dominic was invited to Littlemore, the residence of John Henry Newman and some of his companions. (By this time Newman had given up his position as pastor of the church of Saint Mary in Oxford.) In Dominic they found the answer to their main problem. Many years later, speaking of their first meeting, Newman said, *When his form came in sight I was moved to the depths in the strangest way. His very look had about it something holy.* Dominic was regarded by all as a friend and guide. A year later Dalgairns finally made his decision to become a Catholic and went to Aston Hall to Dominic to be received. Newman was moved by the change in his friend: *If you could see how changed and happy Dalgairns is, you would wonder. I cannot describe it, but it is the manner of a person entrusted with a great gift.* Shortly afterwards, Dominic was again invited to Littlemore, where John Henry Newman was praying to see his own way forward. He felt that Dominic's visit was God's answer to his prayer; he knew of his vocation to work for the conversion of England, and asked Dominic to receive him into the Catholic Church. This was one of the happiest moments in the life of each; Dominic had prayed so much for his conversion, and so many other souls were to follow this man who was to become a Cardinal, and whose process of beatification is now under way. Newman had finally come home. Two of his friends were received by Dominic at the same time, making their first Holy Communion during the Mass he celebrated for them. Newman's conversion had considerable repercussions; he was highly respected as a man of great culture and intellect, vastly influential among the Anglicans. Over thirty Anglican clergymen followed him into the Catholic church. On being informed by Cardinal Wiseman of Newman's conversion, Pope Gregory XVI sent him his special apostolic blessing and commended Dominic, who spared no pains that he might lead straying sheep to the one fold of Christ.

Faith and trust

Dominic's trust in Divine Providence was proverbial. If some project was needed for the good of souls, he invariably put it into operation without worrying where to find the money to finance it. His philosophy was that the funds at the disposal of Divine Providence are great. Divine Providence will never go bankrupt. His students also learned to have complete trust in him. One of them, a young man named Bernard, was found to be suffering from advanced tuberculosis. The doctors said that nothing could be done for him. One lung was no longer functioning, the other was infected. They gave him no more than two or three months to live. Fr Dominic was sent for to help him prepare for death. On Dominic's entering the room, Bernard made a surprising request – *Please cure me*. Dominic replied that he *could not work miracles*; he paused for a moment, then said, *If it be the will of God*, making the sign of the Cross with his thumb on the young man's forehead. Soon afterwards, Dominic had to return to the monastery. On the way out he said to Bernard, *Well, are you going to die?* The other replied, *Father, I shall not die, but live*, to which Dominic added with great feeling, *and narrate the wonderful works of God*. Bernard lived for many more years.

Unswerving loyalty to the spirit of the Passionists' founder, Saint Paul of the Cross, was another of Dominic's outstanding traits. He suffered intensely when some of the monks wanted to mitigate their austere lives as they feared that possible vocations might be deterred. In England they could wear the habit and sandals only within their own territory (due to anti-Catholic laws still in force). Some however wished to abandon the wearing of sandals altogether. Dominic felt that once they gave way on this, other relaxations of the rule would creep in and the Passionist spirit would no longer be as God had shown it to their founder. It was not until after Dominic's death that his fidelity to their rule was fully appreciated, and precautions were taken to prevent innovations which would debilitate it. Some time before he died Dominic was asked if he would pray for the Passionists from heaven. His reply was, *If God in his mercy one day calls me to Heaven, I will ask him to preserve the Congregation as long as it maintains the rule, but not otherwise.*

Death

Death was not something Dominic ever feared. Answering someone who told him she was afraid of the particular Judgement, Dominic with tears in his eyes exclaimed, *Oh, but how sweet to see for the first time the Sacred Humanity of Jesus!* His own death came when he was on a train journey, on August the 27th, 1849, on his way to the opening of a new church. Another priest was travelling with him. When he was suddenly taken ill, a doctor on the train diagnosed a severe heart attack. The priest and the doctor took him off at the next station and went to a nearby cottage, where they had to lay him on the floor. As there was an epidemic of cholera at the time no-one was willing to let him stay, so they took him on another train back towards Reading. Before their departure, Dominic, who was in great pain, made his confession and received absolution. He was placed on some straw on the floor of the guard's van, suffering with each jolt of the train. He spoke only to give thanks to God for his priest companion, and to say, *Lord, if this is what You desire, may Your Will be done.* The doctor found a place for him in the Railway Tavern at Reading, and took his leave, assuring the priest that Dominic would recover and promising to return in three hours. Dominic died in great pain, but with joy, accompanied by the priest, offering his life and his death for the conversion of his beloved stray sheep.

He was finally buried under the high altar of Saint Anne's church, Sutton, and was beatified on the 27th of October 1963. His feast is celebrated on the 26th of August.

BLESSED EDITH STEIN

SISTER TERESA BENEDICTA
OF THE CROSS

Edith, the youngest child in the family of Siegfried and Augusta Stein, was born on 12th October 1891 in the German city of Breslau (now Wroclaw, in Poland). Both parents were pious Jews, and for them the fact that their youngest daughter was born on Yom Kippur, the Day of Atonement, was of great significance. But they little suspected what lay ahead in God's plans for the child.

Four of their family had died in infancy and an even greater sorrow came when Siegfried died suddenly from sunstroke when only forty-eight. The baby, Edith, was only two years old. Augusta rose to the occasion and, in addition to caring for her family, took charge of the timber business which had been run by her husband. Edith grew up, a vivacious, intelligent child, with a very pronounced will of her own. The eldest daughter Elisa helped her mother with the education of the little ones, until in 1897 Edith asked and was allowed to go to school. She loved to read, was not so enthusiastic about mathematics, and took part in all the extra-curricular activities. When she was thirteen, Edith left school for a few months to live in Hamburg helping her sister Elisa, who was then married with three small children. Although she did not enjoy housework, Edith was very conscientious, had a great spirit of service, and fulfilled all her tasks cheerfully. She then resumed her studies and passed the entrance exam for Breslau University with the highest marks. The course she chose, German language and literature included philosophy, which Edith found fascinating and absorbing.

While still at school she had begun to lose interest in religion, and now, at university, she no longer believed in a personal God, although when she was at home she would accompany her mother to the synagogue to avoid making her suffer. Edith's companions found her very friendly and loyal, always ready to help others and share in their joys and sorrows. She hoped to become a teacher, and as well as being very gifted intellectually, possessed the necessary qualities of tact, patience and an ability to get on with everyone, especially children.

Contact with Catholicism

The works of the philosopher Edmund Husserl (1853-1938) made a great impact on Edith, to such an extent that in 1912 she transferred from Breslau to Gottingen where she would be able to attend his lectures. Husserl had a new approach to philosophy – phenomenology – and was considered the greatest philosopher of his time, becoming a Nobel prize-winner. A young tutor in the department, Adolf Reinach, introduced Edith to *the Master*. Edith finished her doctoral thesis in 1916 and became Husserl's assistant in Freiburg. Despite her great esteem for Husserl, Edith disagreed with his *Ideas for a Pure Phenomenology*, realizing that this philosophy too, was in fact subjective. Around this time she attended a lecture by Max Scheler, a Jewish convert to Catholicism who was enthralled by the beauty of his new-found faith. Scheler impressed Edith greatly, as did her friends Adolf

Reinach and his wife, both of whom had been converted to Christianity. When Adolf died in Flanders in 1917, his widow asked Edith to help sort out his philosophy papers, to which Edith readily agreed, happy to do anything to help her friend in her bereavement. The example of her friend's supernatural reaction to Adolf's death came as a revelation to Edith. Later she wrote *It was then that I first encountered the Cross, and the divine strength which it inspires in those who bear it.* From that moment Edith began to read the new Testament, and discovered something which surpassed all she had looked for in her philosophical studies. Her problem of faith continued for several years, during which she returned to Breslau to carry on her work of teaching and investigation.

Conversion

It was in the summer of 1921 while spending the holidays with her friends Hedwig Conrad-Martius and her husband that Edith saw clearly that the Catholic faith was the truth she had been seeking. One evening, when alone in the house, she picked up by chance the autobiography of Saint Teresa of Avila. She spent the night reading it from cover to cover. When she finished, Edith told herself, *This is the truth!* She went out and bought a catechism and a missal, studied both thoroughly and went for the first time to Holy Mass. After Mass, she approached the priest and, to his surprise, asked to be baptized there and then. He explained that she would need more time for preparation and the date for her baptism was fixed for the following year, January 1st, 1922. In the meantime, Edith attended Holy Mass each day and, on her return to Breslau, went to speak to a priest there, Professor Günther Schulemann, who, among other things, advised her to study the writings of Saint Thomas Aquinas. He was very much struck by Edith's docility. On the day of her baptism Edith also received Our Lord for the first time. The name she chose for her baptism was that of the saint who had helped her to discover the Church – Teresa. Edith knew that her decision would not be understood by her family, particularly her mother; she was almost, in fact, expecting to be rejected. Rather than informing her mother by letter, she chose to tell her personally. Kneeling in front of her, Edith told her gently and clearly, *Mother, I am a Catholic*. She had not expected her mother's reaction. Frau Stein had faced so many sufferings and difficulties, and had never been seen to cry, but now she wept. Without fully understanding, she felt that this was the Will of God, which she accepted despite her grief. As one of Edith's Catholic friends wrote, *I am convinced that the change which had taken place in Edith and which lit up her whole being with supernatural radiance disarmed Frau Stein. As a God-fearing woman, she sensed, without realizing it, the holiness radiating from her daughter, and though her suffering was excruciating, she clearly recognized her helplessness before the mystery of grace.* Frau Stein even commented later, *I have never seen anyone pray like Edith.*

Edith was confirmed in Speyer on February 2nd, the feast of the Presentation of Our Lord, and it was there that she met Canon Schwind, who was to be her spiritual director for some time. Her greatest desire was to give her life entirely to God by joining an enclosed order of nuns, but the Canon advised her to continue her work of teaching and philosophical research. He suggested that she should take a post in the Dominican teacher-training college of Saint Mary Magdalene. The years spent there in Speyer helped

Edith to deepen in her interior life and quietly help other souls to come closer to Christ. One of the nuns said of her, *In humility and simplicity, almost unheard and unnoticed, she went quietly about her duties, always serenely friendly and accessible to anyone who wanted her help ... God alone can know to how many people she gave help, advice and direction, how often she came as an angel of charity to the relief of spiritual and corporal need.* Time was always found by her to visit and help anyone, especially the poor. Love for one's neighbour was for Edith an end in itself, because God is Love.

Canon Schwind died suddenly in 1927 while hearing confessions. Edith was always grateful to him for the spiritual guidance he had given her. In 1928 she spent Holy Week at the Benedictine Abbey at Beuron. The Abbot, Fr Waltzer, became her next confessor and director. He too advised her to continue her professional work as a means of helping others at the same time maintaining her union with God. Someone who saw her praying at the Abbey remarked, *Today, I think Edith has not only meditated on the Passion, but has also had a presentiment that she too will have to travel along the road of the Passion.* Prayer was an essential part of her day; *It is necessary,* she wrote, *to have a silent corner in which to converse with God as if nothing else existed, every day. The early morning seems to me to be best for this, before the day's work begins. Further, one should in that quiet place accept one's special mission, preferably each day, and not to choose it oneself. Finally one should see oneself entirely as an instrument, and those powers with which one chiefly has to work as something that we do not use ourselves, but which God uses in us.* She always considered Our Lady, the Handmaid of the Lord, as the perfect example for everyone who wants to fulfil God's Will.

Her services were frequently required as a lecturer on religious, educational and philosophical themes in Germany, Austria and Poland, and after her lecture on *The proper dignity of women and its place in the life of the nation*, her reputation as a speaker was even further enhanced. In 1932 she became a Professor at Munster. In the midst of all this work, in her spare time she translated the *Questiones disputatae de Veritate* of Saint Thomas Aquinas (*Disputed Questions concerning Truth*) into German. This was published in two volumes in 1931-32. Her study of the writings of Saint Thomas opened up new horizons for Edith in the field of philosophy and in her relationship with God. Like Saint Thomas, Edith found the strength to carry out all her duties by spending time in prayer before the Tabernacle.

The beginning of persecution

For some time Edith had been very keenly aware of anti-Jewish feeling in her country. The climax was reached when in 1933 Hitler set up the Third Reich. Edith felt very deeply for her people – *You cannot imagine what it means to me to be a daughter of the Chosen People, to belong to Christ not only spiritually, but also by blood*. She foresaw the impending tragedy before most of her contemporaries were aware of it. During Holy Week she saw that Our Lord wanted her to share in carrying his Cross. How, she did not know, but offered herself for whatever God wanted, as a means of making reparation to him. In her concern for the Jewish people she wrote to the Holy Father and received a letter in reply, giving his blessing to her and her family. On the 23rd of February 1933 Edith's career as a lecturer came to an end. Because of the new legislation, Jews were no longer able to hold public office. At the same time she was offered a post in South America. Edith, however, saw that this was the moment to ask permission to join the Carmelite Order. Fr Waltzer agreed. Edith could no longer influence Catholic life; her mother also would be more easily resigned to having her in a convent in Cologne rather than far away in South America. She was accepted by the Carmelites in Cologne in June 1933. Edith thanked God for drawing so much good from such great evil. The parting with her mother and family was very hard; they did not understand. Her mother, weeping, asked, *Why did you have to know him? I don't want to say anything against him. I admit that He was a good man, but why did He make himself God?* Edith recalled the words of Our Lord, *None of you can be my disciple if he does not take leave of all that he possesses.*(Luke 14:33) Speaking of her departure from her mother, Edith said, *I had to take this step totally in the darkness of faith.* She was already learning to share in the Cross. At the time her family did not understand that this separation and Edith's future life were to bring many blessings upon them and all their afflicted people. On the 14th of October Edith entered the convent.

Sister Teresa Benedicta of the Cross

Life there was a complete contrast to what had been the life of a well-known university lecturer. Edith was the most recent postulant, but was about twenty years older than the rest. She was very unskilled in housework, cooking and sewing, and had much to learn from the younger nuns. In her humility, Edith was filled with happiness and fitted into her new surroundings perfectly. April 15th, 1934 was the day she received the habit and chose the name *Teresa Benedicta*

of the Cross (combining her baptismal name, her gratitude to the Benedictines who had guided her, and the
Cross which she wished to carry with Our Lord). She
joyfully gave her all – family, friends, profession, fame
– to become God's humble instrument. One of her
companions spoke of the inspiration she had been to
them, knowing who she was, to see her whole-hearted
self-giving, naturalness, joy and simplicity, but especially her spirit of prayer. Edith lived her Carmelite
vocation with great love and finesse, offering up the
things that cost her most, adapting herself to convent
life when already over forty, and to the household
duties to which she was unaccustomed. Everything
became a means for her of drawing closer to God. Her
joy, peace and gratitude for all the graces she received
were noticed by the other sisters and friends who
visited her from time to time.

Soon, Edith was asked by her superiors to resume
her literary activities. She completed her work *Finite
Being and Eternal Being*, and produced a study of Saint
John of the Cross. In 1936 Frau Stein died, still not
fully understanding her daughter's vocation, but after
visiting a Carmelite convent she had once more started
to write to Edith. The same year Edith had the joy of
giving some final classes to her sister Rosa and attending her Baptism. Rosa made her first Holy Communion on Christmas night. Like Edith, Rosa too saw that
she had a vocation to be a Carmelite.

Edith made her final vows in 1938, the year in
which Hitler promulgated further repressive laws
against the Jewish people. All Jews were obliged to
give an account of their possessions, to add the name
Israel in their passport, to add a *J* to their travel documents; women had to put *Sarah*. The civil authorities
lost little time in discovering that the Convent in

Cologne was sheltering Jewish nuns. Arrangements were made by the nuns for Edith to *have a change of air* and go to Echt in Holland for safety. In 1940 she was joined by Rosa, who had escaped through Belgium.

In Echt, Edith immediately adapted to her new surroundings, learning Dutch (her seventh language) and made a great effort to be a help – sometimes with amusing results, as can be seen from what was later written of her by the nuns. *From the very first day Sister Benedicta tried to adapt herself to the community's customs. Ever ready to help and wishing to share in all the work, she never refused any favours that were asked of her. Often, in fact, she even got in the way through over-eagerness because with all the good will in the world she could never make a thorough job of being practical ... In recreation she was at once serious and cheerful, though she could laugh heartily and was always glad to tell stories about her interesting life.*

Once again Edith was requested to write, one of her outstanding works of this period being *The Science of the Cross*. Shortly before the outbreak of World War II Edith had written to her superior asking permission to offer herself to God. *Allow me to offer myself as a victim in reparation to the Sacred Heart of Jesus, for true peace, so that the power of the Antichrist may be defeated as soon as possible without another war, and that a new order may be established in the world. I know that I am nothing, but Jesus wants it and during these days He is going to call many other souls for the same purpose.*

As if she already knew of her impending death, Edith also made her will on the Friday after Corpus Christi; in it she wrote, *From now on I accept the death which God has destined for me, with complete submission to his most Holy Will, and with joy. I ask Our Lord to accept my life and death for his renown and glory, for all the intentions of the Most Sacred Hearts of Jesus and Mary, of Holy Church, especially for the preservation, sanctification and perfection of our Order, particularly the convents of Cologne and Echt, to make reparation for the disbelief of the Jewish people, that Our Lord may be accepted by his own, and his glorious kingdom come; for the salvation of Germany and the peace of the whole world; finally for my relations, living and dead, and for all those whom God has given me, so that none of them may be lost.* Knowing that all suffering can, since the Crucifixion of Christ, be incorporated into his Passion and Death, she saw that the heavy cross of the destruction of the people of Israel could become the sign of redemption if accepted in union with his suffering.

With the Nazi invasion of Holland in 1940 many atrocities were committed against the Jews; they were excluded from public life and, by 1942, mass deportations started. Many were sent to concentration camps in Poland, others to labour in the mines or to the gas chambers. All Jews in Holland were ordered to wear a yellow star of David on their garments. In sympathy and as a protest against this measure, many Dutch citizens also wore the yellow star, but to no avail. The Catholic hierarchy of Holland issued a joint pastoral letter which contained the text of a telegram they had sent to the authorities deploring the treatment of the Jewish citizens. In reprisal, orders were given on the 2nd of August for the arrest of all non-Aryan members of Dutch religious communities. The Nazi Commandant announced the same day that this was because of the pastoral letter, saying *We are compelled to regard the Catholic Jews as our worst enemies, and consequently to see to their deportation to the East with all possible speed.*

Arrest and deportation

The nuns in Echt had planned to send the two Stein sisters to the Convent of Le Paquier in Switzerland. Travel documents were applied for, but took a long time to arrive. Edith had not long to wait for the acceptance of the offering of her life and death.

At 5 p.m. on August 2nd, 1941, the doorbell of the convent rang. Two officers of the SS stood at the door. At first the Prioress thought they had come about the travel permit. She was soon undeceived. Edith and Rosa were given ten minutes in which to prepare to leave. The Prioress did all she could on their behalf, and was threatened with reprisals against the community. Edith went to the chapel and asked the Sisters for their prayers, then sorrowfully took her leave.

In the meantime a crowd had gathered outside, outraged by this new act of violence, but helpless to do anything to prevent it. The two sisters were hustled into the waiting van, together with other victims, and driven off rapidly to Amersfort concentration camp. One of the occupants of the van saw how Edith took her sister's hand, saying, *Come on, let us offer ourselves in sacrifice for our people.* In Amersfort they received brutal treatment, being beaten with rifle butts and forced to the dormitories where they were imprisoned without food. Two survivors related how Edith spoke up bravely on behalf of the other women in the camp, most of whom were almost in despair. They never forgot how Edith and the other members of religious orders accepted their situation with calm and peace. Among the three hundred Catholic prisoners, fifteen were religious; they met together to say the office and the rosary, taking Edith as their Superior. After a few days, twelve hundred of the prisoners, including the two Steins, were transferred to Westerbork, where Edith

was able to send a brief message to the convent at Echt
– to the effect that they had time to pray all day. In
Westerbork, families were separated with no possibility
of communicating with each other. They were constantly harassed by interrogations, each one of them
being photographed with their camp number. In the
midst of the desolation and panic, Edith brought calm
and hope to others. She took care of the children,
washed them and combed their hair; she consoled and
comforted the other women. One of those who lived
said of her: *My personal impression is that she was most
deeply sorrowful, but without anxiety ... She was thinking of the sorrows she foresaw for others, not of her own
sorrow – she was far too calm for that. She thought of
all the grief that lay ahead. Her whole appearance, as I
picture her in my memory, sitting in that hut, suggested
only one thought to me; a Pietá without Christ.*

On the 6th of August Edith sent a short note to
the convent at Echt to say that they were leaving the
next day for Siberia or Czechoslovakia. During the
night they were suddenly awakened. A list was read of
those who had to prepare to leave. Only six men were
left. By dawn, long lines of men, women and children,
among them the religious, in their habits, moved in sin-
gle file towards the wagons which would take them
away. The train stopped for a while in the station of
Schiffenstadt. On the platform was a former pupil of
Edith's, recently married. She heard someone calling
her by her maiden name. To her surprise and dismay
she saw Edith standing at one of the barred windows of
the prison train. Edith called out, *Give my love to the
Sisters at Saint Mary Magdalene. I am going East.*

Their destination was reached on the 9th of
August – Auschwitz. As the trains pulled in, a process
of selection took place. Those who were physically fit

and under fifty years of age were sent to the work camps. Edith, fifty-one, was slightly built; Rosa was fifty-nine, so they were among those told they were to be *disinfected*. They all knew that this meant the gas chamber. Many of the Jews went to their death singing psalms. Their bodies were afterwards thrown into a common ditch. In such a way as this Edith fulfilled her sacrifice, undergoing bitter humiliation and untold suffering. She never lost her supernatural serenity, joyfully offering everything to win her people for Christ and to make reparation to his Sacred Heart.

Edith Stein, Sister Teresa Benedicta of the Cross, was beatified by Pope John Paul II in May 1987 during his visit to Germany.

SAINT ELIZABETH SETON

Early childhood

On the 28th of August 1774 a second child was born to Catherine, the wife of Richard Bayley, a young New York doctor. The baby was christened Elizabeth in the Episcopalian church of which Catherine was a member. When Mary's and Elizabeth's new sister was born three years later, their mother died. Richard named the baby Catherine in memory of his wife. He married again a year later; his second wife, Charlotte, was still in her teens and in addition to all the duties she undertook as a doctor's wife she had to take care of the three girls, all under six years of age. Catherine, the youngest, was very delicate and died before she was two.

Elizabeth was deeply affected, although not perhaps in the way that might have been expected. She was found sitting on the porch steps next to the tiny coffin, looking up at the sky. When asked why it was that with her little sister dead she was not crying, she replied, *Because Kitty has gone to Heaven; I wish I could go to Heaven to be with my mother too*. Her mother, a devout Episcopalian, had often talked to Mary and Elizabeth about God and about how they too would one day go to Heaven. Richard found little time for religion, dedicating himself to his medical work, much of which he devoted to caring for the poor and destitute.

By 1783 George Washington was President of a new nation. The colonial rule of Britain was at an end.

The Bayleys became American citizens.

Like her father, Elizabeth even when very young loved to take care of others. She helped to look after her seven step-brothers and sisters for whom she had great affection. Charlotte was rather reserved towards Mary and Elizabeth, and when the latter was eight Richard decided to send the pair of them to his brother William in New Rochelle for several months. The two Bayley children were very happy there and immediately felt part of the family, now having four cousins as companions. When they returned home their father made sure that great attention was paid to their education. In addition to other subjects, Richard insisted on their learning French and studying music, neither of which Elizabeth liked but which proved to be a great asset in later life.

Her impulsive character was similar to that of her father, who helped her to obtain mastery over herself and to put the needs of others before her own. His example was highly effective. When requested one day by another surgeon for his assistance in a complicated operation, he excused himself by saying that he was tired and had many other things to do. Disappointed, the other mentioned how reluctant he himself was to refuse, as the family of his patient were poor. Instantly Dr Bayley said, *Let's go at once. Why didn't you tell me at first that they were poor?*

For professional reasons Dr Bayley left for England in 1788, leaving his two elder daughters with their relatives in New Rochelle. Elizabeth missed him a great deal and later wrote that she found consolation in the thought that God is our Father. Her habit of prayer, acquired in childhood, was of great assistance in her difficult moments. She had also begun to read a little from the Bible every day – another custom which she retained.

When Dr Bayley returned home three years later he and Elizabeth grew to understand each other better and a close bond was formed between them. Mary was by now married, and Elizabeth had an active social life, with many friends; she was popular because of her open, affectionate nature, her gentleness and her integrity. Around this period in her life she felt the urge to gather many children around her so that she could teach and care for them.

William Seton

Among the people she met was a young man of Scottish descent, William Magee Seton, the son of a wealthy ship-owner. William had been educated in Europe, where he had travelled widely. During the course of his work in Italy he had become a close friend of the Filicchi family, who were Catholic. Their life, consistent as it was with their beliefs, made a lasting impression on William, who like Elizabeth was a Protestant. The two young people became engaged in 1792 and married in the Episcopalian church in 1794 when Elizabeth was twenty. Their marriage was happy and they welcomed the birth of Anna María in 1795 and of William in the following year. The Seton shipping business prospered and the couple were well thought of in New York society. Elizabeth's father-in-law resembled her own father in his concern for the poor and, following the example of their generosity, she also made time to help those in need. Together with other influential ladies, she started an organisation to assist needy widows. She and her sister-in-law Rebecca became very close friends, and Rebecca took part in the charitable work.

With the sudden death of William's father, the

burden of the family responsibilities fell on him. He had to take care of his younger brothers and sisters at a time when the firm was passing through a period of instability. Elizabeth quietly became a pillar of strength for William, taking over the management of the large Seton house and dealing with much of the complicated paperwork, while remaining all the time very much in the background. Their second son, Richard, was born about this time, to be followed by another daughter, Catherine. Elizabeth took upon herself the education of Harriet and Cecilia, the two younger Seton girls, in addition to that of her own children.

In summer the family moved to Staten Island for the holidays with Elizabeth's father. Dr Bayley had been fully occupied that year attending those suffering from an epidemic of yellow fever. Then he too contracted the disease. Elizabeth remained by his bedside constantly; her sister Mary's husband, a doctor too, did all he could, but the end was very near. Elizabeth's constant concern was for her father's soul. He had professed no religious belief and she prayed earnestly for his salvation. Her prayers were not in vain. During the last hours of his life, Dr Bayley constantly murmured *May Christ Jesus have mercy on me!* He died less than a week after catching the fever.

The little family increased to five with the birth of another Rebecca, but Elizabeth's happiness was clouded by the realisation that her husband was showing symptoms of tuberculosis, a fatal illness at that time. Thinking that a change of climate would be beneficial, the Setons arranged to visit the Filicchis in Livorno. They left America for Italy in October 1803, taking Anna Maria, their eight-year-old daughter, with them and leaving the younger children with their relations. The journey took six weeks and, to their distress, when they got there the port authorities put them into quarantine; having heard of the yellow fever epidemic they assumed that William had the disease. The accommodation in the *Lazaretto* left much to be desired. It was cold, damp, draughty and unfurnished. The Filicchis immediately sent food, bedding and one of their servants to attend them, but because of the conditions William's health deteriorated rapidly. Elizabeth and Anna María attempted to keep warm by using the cord from one of their travel-trunks as a skipping-rope. In her diary, Elizabeth wrote: *This is the time of trial. In permitting it Our Lord gives us support and strength.* A few days later the entry reads: *Not only willing to take my cross, but kissed it too.*

After a month that seemed eternal they were allowed to leave. The Filicchis had rented a house for them, providing also whatever else they thought they might need, and sent their carriage to collect them. William soon began to recover, but by Christmas he was again failing noticeably. He died aged thirty-five. Elizabeth, herself not thirty, found herself a widow in a foreign country and without resources. The affairs of his firm were in a far worse state than William had realised; Elizabeth tactfully had not let him know they were almost bankrupt.

Searching for the truth

The Filicchis – Filippo and his English wife Mary, and Antonio, whose wife Amabilia was also Italian – did all in their power to make the bereaved mother and her little girl welcome. For the Italian family, their religion was an integral part of life; they spoke to Elizabeth quite naturally about their faith, which had a fascination for her. Filippo told her one day that everyone has the duty to seek the true religion, through praying to know the truth, and then to follow it. Elizabeth, who had great confidence in him, said she supposed he wanted her to pray, search, and then embrace the Catholic faith. She was somewhat surprised by Filippo's reply, which left her free from any feeling of compulsion: *I only ask that you will pray and search.*

Antonio Filicchi also gently encouraged her to find out more about the Catholic religion. Filippo showed her one day how to make the sign of the Cross and its significance. She wrote in her diary, *I was cold with the awe-filled impression my first making it gave me – the sign of the Cross of Christ on me! Deepest thoughts came with it of I know not what earnest desires to be closely united with him who died on it.*

A realisation of the Real Presence of Christ in the Blessed Sacrament occurred when, with the Filicchis, she visited a shrine of Our Lady and attended Mass with them there. Just before the elevation, an English tourist commented mockingly, *This is what they call their Real Presence*. A tremor went through her. The words of Saint Paul flashed upon her mind … *not discerning the Body of the Lord*. She then thought – if He is not truly present, how could Saint Paul say … *he is eating and drinking damnation to himself if he eats and drinks unworthily, not recognizing the Lord's Body for what It is* (1 Cor 11:29).

Later, when the Blessed Sacrament was being carried through the street past the house, she instantly fell to her knees, praying in anguish, asking God to bless her if He were truly present. Another step towards her conversion came when she found in one of the prayer-books in the house a prayer to Our Lady, asking her to be our Mother. Elizabeth read it, convinced that God would not refuse his Mother anything – she felt she had indeed found a Mother.

When Elizabeth and Anna María travelled back to America, Antonio accompanied them. Elizabeth attended Mass on the ship and continued to read and enquire about Catholicism. Her friends had warned her to prepare to meet difficulties if she decided to become a Catholic. Filippo gave her a letter of introduction to Archbishop John Carroll to facilitate matters, but for some reason Elizabeth did not make use of it.

She went first to a close friend of her family, John Hobart, a zealous Protestant minister. She also rather imprudently informed her family and friends of her desire to become a Catholic, little realising what their reaction would be. Her grasp of the Catholic faith was no match for the objections put forward by John Hobart; she became confused and disturbed. Antonio Filicchi, still in America, advised her to speak to a holy priest whom he knew, Fr John Chevenus. Elizabeth went to him early in 1805 and explained her position. Fr Chevenus enabled her to overcome the remaining obstacles and told her she should make her decision soon, and if any doubt arose in her mind she should make an act of faith – *I believe. Lord, help my unbelief!*

The effect of this spiritual guidance was remarkable. Ten days after her first interview with Fr Chevenus, Elizabeth was received into the Church. She had learned the hard way how necessary it is for the soul to have a spiritual director to act as a guide, leading it to God, encouraging it in the struggle to overcome defects and grow in virtue. In a letter to Amabilia, she wrote of her first Confession: *I saw only Our Lord himself in the priest who represented him in the Sacrament of Mercy. Oh, how beautiful are these words of absolution which broke the chains of thirty years of bondage!*

On the 25th of March, the Feast of the

Annunciation, she received Our Lord for the first time. Later, she wrote: *In Holy Communion our hearts are the Tabernacle of the Divinity. We should carefully guard the casket containing so precious a jewel.*

Elizabeth found herself in the position of having to support her children with no income whatsoever. As soon as the Filicchis knew of her plight, they immediately came to her aid as did Mary and her husband, and a grateful friend, John Wilkes, whose dying wife had been tended by Elizabeth during her last illness. Elizabeth, however, was determined to earn her own living and sought a teaching post where she could be with her children. She joined the staff of a recently-opened school, started by an English couple, but there were too few pupils to make it viable. Mr Wilkes again came to the rescue and, with Elizabeth, set up a small boarding-school. She began a busy life of teaching and keeping the children occupied in the evenings – thinking with gratitude how her father had insisted so much on her learning French and music.

She was surprised to find how strong were the anti-Catholic sentiments of most of her family and friends. Harriet and Cecilia, her sisters-in-law remained very loyal as did two of her step-sisters, Mary and Helen. Cecilia then disclosed to her that she too wanted to become a Catholic, keeping her decision from the rest of the family until she had received sufficient instruction in the faith and was ready to be received.

At this point she informed the others, who were outraged, putting the blame on Elizabeth. When Cecilia persevered firmly despite all opposition and became a Catholic, life was made almost impossible for Elizabeth. She was instantly disinherited by some of her relatives, parents removed their daughters from the school, and an active campaign of persecution began. The Filicchis, who had already done so much, invited Elizabeth to go to Italy, but she decided to weather the storm and stay in New York.

The Foundress

After Mass one day Elizabeth approached the priest, Fr Du Bourg, who happened to be on a visit from Boston. She told him of her awkward situation and of her desire to teach children. Having thought over the matter and discussed it with other priests, he suggested that she could not only set up a Catholic school for girls in Baltimore – there were already three for boys – but also that she should found a women's religious association for the purpose of education. Bishop Carroll was fully in agreement with the proposal and in 1808 Elizabeth and her children left New York for Baltimore. Time had healed the rift with some of her relations and Cecilia was able to follow her own plan to join Elizabeth at a later date.

The beginnings in Baltimore were very small – seven pupils to start with, of which three were Elizabeth's own daughters. It was a seed destined to grow beyond all expectations. A young woman, Cecilia O'Conner, who had heard of the undertaking and who, like Elizabeth, felt she had a religious vocation, came to join her. As there was very little money and as Elizabeth's family were all still of school age and needing their mother, the obstacles to her becoming a religious or starting the teaching project seemed insurmountable. Both Elizabeth and Cecilia O'Conner continued to pray, and an answer came very quickly in the form of a generous offer from a convert who was willing to finance the school and also requested them to care for the elderly and the poor. The convent and school were to be in Emmitsburg, where Mount Saint Mary's college for boys had already been established.

On the fourth anniversary of her first Holy Communion, the 25th of March 1809, Elizabeth became a religious and the foundress of the first American religious community. Other vocations came very soon; together with Elizabeth the newcomers promised to dedicate themselves to assisting the poor, the sick and all in need, especially children. The new Sisters of Charity were joined in Emmitsburg by Cecilia Seton, the convert, and her sister Harriet, a Protestant, who was struggling within herself to decide whether to remain in the religion of her family, or take the enormous step of becoming a Catholic.

Like so many others, she turned trustingly to Elizabeth. Together they walked to the church to pray before the Blessed Sacrament. When they came out, Harriet had made up her mind; Elizabeth advised her not to act hastily, but Harriet was firm – she became a Catholic in September 1809. The grace of her conversion was to become a consolation in sorrow for Elizabeth: Harriet fell gravely ill two months later and died shortly before Christmas. Cecilia Seton too died the following April. Elizabeth saw here in practice the urgent need of always helping souls to find the truth, as one never knew if there would be a second opportunity. She felt very deeply that she had received an infinite treasure and, as God's instrument, had to share this with many others.

Her confident, absolute trust in God was very evident during the difficulties faced by the new community. Contradictions and misunderstandings arose from well-meaning good people; a number of the Sisters were ill, funds were lacking – and at times their food was extremely scarce. A nearby spring was the only source of drinking water, which had to be brought to the house in buckets; the washing had to be done in the river. All this Elizabeth offered willingly to God, always retaining her gentle good humour. The fruits of the sacrifice were not long in coming. By 1810 the number of Sisters and of those who wished to join exceeded the capacity of the convent. In February they moved to a larger building, which they put under the patronage of Saint Joseph; in addition to the boarding school, which was flourishing, a free school for children of the neighbourhood was started. The Sisters always found time as well to visit the homes of those in need.

The Constitutions, given to the nuns by the Archbishop in 1812, were based on the rule of the Congregation founded by Saint Vincent de Paul. Provision was made for Elizabeth to take care of her children as long as was necessary. The first Sister to be admitted after they received the Constitutions was Anna Maria, Elizabeth's eldest daughter. She had prayed earnestly for Anna Maria's vocation, but in order to leave her totally free had never actively encouraged it. Again, her joy was seasoned with sorrow; Anna Maria, aged sixteen at the time, was already a victim of tuberculosis. She died in March 1812, two months after becoming a member of the community.

Numbers continued to grow; Elizabeth gave herself unstintingly to her nuns, the teachers whom she trained, the pupils and all the poor people living in the area. Thanks to her prayers, example and effort there were numerous conversions. Constantly occupied with all her duties, she never made visitors feel they were interrupting her; a smile welcomed each one as if she had no concern other than to attend to them. New foundations were initiated in 1814 – an orphanage in Philadelphia followed shortly by a school, and a further enterprise in New York.

Elizabeth's life of prayer, work and sacrifice was a source of inspiration and encouragement to those who met her. Her supernatural approach to suffering enabled her to bear and offer lovingly the many sorrows she had to undergo. There was never a trace of self-pity. She would say, *You think you make a sacrifice. Look at the Sacrifice of Calvary and compare yours to it.* When in 1816 her youngest child Rebecca died at fourteen from a tumour caused by a fall, Elizabeth was able to offer her daughter to God, thanking him for taking her to Heaven. Her own death was not far off. Like many members of her family, she too eventually contracted tuberculosis. Having received the Sacraments, she died peacefully on the 4th of January 1821, at the age of forty-six, repeating the names of Jesus, Mary and Joseph.

The effects of her life have continued to help countless souls – her daughter Catherine also became a religious, and one of her grandsons a priest. The religious community she founded kept up her work in education and among the sick and those in distress. She was canonized by Pope Paul VI in 1975; her feast is kept on the 4th of January.

Saint Jean-Marie Baptiste Vianney

The Curé of Ars

On the 8th of May, 1786, three years before the French Revolution, Jean-Marie Baptiste Vianney was born in Dardilly, near Lyons in France. His family were farmers. Jean-Marie was the fourth child. During the Revolution and in the years that followed they all remained true to their Faith, attending Mass celebrated in secret by the courageous priests who were loyal to the Pope.

The Vianney home frequently sheltered one of these priests who were hunted with so much hatred by the revolutionaries. They had also given food and lodgings to Saint Benedict Joseph Labré, the beggar who became a saint, some years before Jean-Marie was born. They treasured a letter written to them by the Saint thanking them for their hospitality.

Because there were so few priests, Jean-Marie was eleven years old when he went to Confession for the first time, and thirteen before he could make his first Holy Communion. This was not in his own village, but in nearby Ecully, and not in the church, which had been closed, but in the closely-shuttered house lent for the purpose. Carts filled with hay were placed in front of the house and were unloaded whilst the first Communion Mass was being celebrated. Sixteen children attended the ceremony that day. Fifty years later Jean-Marie still had the rosary which had been given to him on that occasion, and which he had used so often.

Farmer, soldier, seminarian

Work on the farm started for him when he was seven. He looked after the sheep until his younger brothers were considered old enough for this task, then helped in the fields and the vineyard. There was very little time for formal education, and Jean-Marie in any case felt no inclination to study. Like his parents, he was a devout Catholic and developed a habit of finding some quiet place in the stables or in the fields where he could pray. He saw how few priests there were, how many souls were in need of teaching and the Sacraments – he felt that God wanted him to be a priest.

There were many difficulties; his father refused his permission as he could not afford to pay the seminary fees for Jean-Marie. Then there was the question of the deficiencies in his education – he knew no Latin and had considerable difficulty in learning. For two years his father steadily refused to agree, until he learned that in Ecully, the priest, Abbé Charles Balley, had started a school in his presbytery for possible candidates to the priesthood. As one of Jean-Marie's aunts lived there, he could stay with his aunt and uncle and attend the classes. M. Balley accepted him and the classes began.

He found the studies, particularly Latin, extremely difficult. Jean-Marie reached the point where he felt like giving up. M. Balley encouraged him, so he decided to make a pilgrimage to the tomb of St Francis Regis at Louvesc in Dauphiné, travelling on foot. He never did overcome the difficulties in learning, but his prayers were answered when at last he became a priest. Before that, he still had to encounter other problems; he became very ill, so had to return home for some time.

When he recovered to go once more to Ecully in

1809, he received call-up papers for the army. Priests and seminarians were exempt, but by some mistake, Jean-Marie's name had been omitted from the list of seminarians. As nothing could be done, Jean-Marie went to the barracks at Lyons, where he became so ill again with fever that he had to be sent to the military hospital. He was discharged after several weeks, not fully recovered, and had to join his detachment, who were on their way to Bayonne for the war against Spain. Because of his weak condition, Jean-Marie never reached them.

Technically, he was a deserter. A stranger, passing along in the same direction, took him to the village of Les Noës, where the Mayor arranged for him to be given shelter and hidden from the search parties sent to round up deserters. When an amnesty was declared, Jean-Marie was able to leave the army, his younger brother agreeing to be his substitute. He was able to return home and be with his mother when she died shortly afterwards.

M. Balley did his best to prepare Jean-Marie, who was accepted at the Lyons Seminary in 1813. He still needed special tuition in Latin, as this was the language in which the classes were given, but nine months later his exam results were so poor that he was dismissed from the seminary. Rather than go home, which would have meant giving up altogether, he went back to Abbé Balley. Thanks to the insight of the priest who believed Jean-Marie truly had a vocation, the Archbishop agreed to take him back.

The great day of his ordination finally arrived on the 13th of August 1815 in Grenoble. By this time he was about thirty. His first appointment was as assistant to Abbé Balley who kept up his instruction. For a while, Jean-Marie was denied the faculty to hear

Confessions, as the Bishop did not consider him competent. When permission was ultimately granted, Abbé Balley asked to be his first penitent. In December 1817 the Abbé died and was greatly missed by his curate.

The new Curé of Ars

Shortly after this Jean-Marie was sent to the village of Ars. It was very small, having only about forty families, and was very much off the beaten track – not the sort of place to which the Bishop would want to send one of his 'good' priests.

Ars had been without a priest for a long time, with the inevitable consequences; the people were, to say the least, indifferent to and ignorant of religion. Life was hard. They sought compensations. They drank heavily. The new Curé began at once to get to know his parishioners, visiting all the families, talking with them, solving problems, encouraging them to attend Sunday Mass. He prepared his sermons with great effort, trying painstakingly to learn them by heart. When the time came for him to preach, he usually forgot what he had tried so hard to learn, and spoke spontaneously of what was in his heart. The congregation listened, and returned to hear him again.

As the church had been neglected, the Curé set out to improve the décor and to ensure that everything was always spotlessly clean – because it was for Our Lord. He bought a new altar, and went on foot to Lyons to purchase the very best vestments and sacred vessels. His faith in the Real Presence of Our Lord in the Blessed Sacrament had more effect on his parishioners than many sermons.

The Curé had very clear in his mind the idea that a priest was for God, and his task was to bring souls to him, instructing them, preparing them for and administering the Sacraments, offering up the Holy Sacrifice on their behalf. He spoke extremely clearly about their need to fulfil the precept of keeping Sunday holy, of avoiding drunkenness and other vices.

He also took care of their material needs – he thought they needed his money, food, furniture more than he did – he could manage on one or two potatoes a day, with the occasional egg. When some poor person needed a bed, the Curé gave away his mattress and slept on planks. He continually practised very severe mortifications to make reparation for sinners.

Gradually the village began to change. Men as well as women began to attend Sunday Mass and frequent the Sacraments; children and adults came to know their Faith, and live it. On the feast of Corpus Christi almost everyone walked in the procession and all the streets were decorated with flowers. In 1854 the entire village shared in the rejoicings at the proclamation of the dogma of the Immaculate Conception; the church bells rang all day and every house was illuminated with candles.

The apostolate of Confession

Some of the priests from neighbouring villages asked the Curé for his help on special occasions; this was the beginning of the ever-increasing number of visitors to Ars who wanted to go to him for confession. News of the country Curé who appeared to have the special gift of 'reading' souls spread further afield. Soon people came from all over France, from other countries in Europe, and waited patiently, sometimes for days, for their turn to go to Confession.

Ars became a kind of tourist attraction because of the Sacrament of Penance. The Curé would spend fifteen or sixteen hours a day in the cramped confessional. He hardly slept. Rising at one o'clock in the morning he would go to the church to pray alone before the Blessed Sacrament. At 6.00 a.m. he celebrated Holy Mass, having already heard some confessions. More confessions followed after Mass until 8.00 a.m., after which he went to one of the houses he had founded for orphaned children, to have a glass of milk. Half an hour later he was back in the confessional until 11.00 a.m. when he gave a catechism class to the children. He stopped at mid-day, went to the house and had his sparse meal. Usually some of the more persistent among the crowd would have managed to slip into the house to speak to him and ask for advice. At 12.30 p.m. he went round to visit any parishioners who were sick, then heard confessions again until 8.00 p.m. This was followed by vespers, a sermon, time spent in private prayer, with further confessions until midnight.

This timetable continued day after day, year after year. There were some who criticised, even among the clergy, and a slanderous campaign was organized against him. A report was prepared for the bishop, listing what were considered his defects and shortcomings; this was circulated among the clergy to collect signatures. By accident, it was sent to the Curé, who read it, added his own signature, and passed it on.

These exterior trials were less of a torment to the Curé than the spiritual aridity, scruples and sense of failure he felt. More than once he felt that the best thing he could do for his people was to leave, as he considered himself such an unworthy priest. He did attempt to leave, but returned each time, overcoming his desire to retire in solitude to a Trappist monastery – too many souls needed him in Ars.

Countless people testified to the fact that he had indeed a supernatural insight into souls, understanding immediately what they were trying to express – and what they had also left unsaid. On numerous occasions he told individuals what their vocation in life was to be – some to married life, others to a religious vocation. His advice was always brief and to the point. The penances he gave were light. When asked why he did this, when perhaps someone had been far from God for many years, he would say that he could not be hard on them, as they had come a great distance and had made many sacrifices to do so – he said that he gave them a small penance and performed the rest for them himself.

Even without speaking to a person, the Curé knew the state of his soul and almost always found the way of touching his heart and helping him go to Confession. One traveller, who only went to Ars to accompany a friend without any intention of confessing his sins, arrived in the village when the Curé was crossing the square. The traveller, who intended to go duck shooting, was carrying his gun and had his retriever dog with him. Suddenly, to his amazement, the Curé stopped in front of him, among all the crowds, and said, *What a pity your soul is not as beautiful as your dog!* The man was amazed and taken aback. The Curé's words made him reflect on his life, and he decided there and then to join the queue for Confession. He was truly repentant; he thought of changing his life completely and was told by the Curé – go to La Trappe. He did so and spent the rest of his days in the enclosed monastery, joyfully following the rule of the Order and eventually dying a holy death.

The Curé showed married people that for them matrimony was the way to sanctity, for themselves and for the rest of their family. He encouraged and also spoke very strongly to one woman awaiting her turn for

Confession. The Curé called her in before her turn; she was expecting another child and was very concerned as she was no longer young. He told her, *Be comforted, my child... If you only knew the women who will go to hell because they did not bring into the world the children they should have given to it!* The following beautiful words were to another mother of a large family. *Come now, my little one, do not be alarmed at your burden; Our Lord carries it with you. The good God does well all that He does. When He gives many children to a young mother it is that He deems her worthy to rear them. It is a mark of confidence on his part.*

Frequent reception of Holy Communion was very much encouraged by the Curé at a time when the influence of Jansenism was still very prevalent. He insisted that those who want to receive Our Lord should prepare themselves well and have an adequate knowledge of the doctrine concerning the Real Presence.

Speaking of Holy Communion in one of his sermons, he told the people: *My children, when God resolved to provide food for our soul so as to sustain her on the pilgrimage of life, He examined the whole of creation, but found nothing that was worthy of her, so He looked at himself and resolved to give himself! O my soul, how great thou art! God alone can satisfy thee! God alone can be the food of the soul! How happy are pure souls that unite themselves to Our Lord in Holy Communion! In Heaven they will sparkle like beautiful diamonds, because God will shine through them. O man, how great thou art! – nourished and refreshed as thou art with the Flesh and Blood of God! Go then to Holy Communion, my children!*

It is not surprising that this work of saving souls angered Satan to the point of his attacking the holy

Curé physically, not just occasionally, but night after night, for years. The devil tried to terrify him by noises and apparitions; the Curé was not the only one to see and hear. One night his bed was set on fire; something was heard beating loudly on the door – but no-one could be seen. The Curé realized after a while that these attacks were most violent just before the arrival of some soul on its way to perdition, so he redoubled his prayers and penances for the salvation of these poor sinners and was able to absolve them, depriving Satan of his prey.

There were so many outstanding conversions and also cures of physical handicaps and diseases that everyone considered them as being due to the prayers of the Curé – which they were. He always attributed them to Saint Philomena and would accept no praise or thanks for himself – telling the people *"to thank the good God."*

In their desire to show appreciation and gratitude, those who had received help from him tried an unusual manner of doing so: he was recommended to the Emperor for the honour of being nominated Chevalier of the Imperial Order of the Legion of Honour. The decoration arrived at Ars – the Curé, who had no desire for worldly recognition never wore it during his lifetime. When he died, they pinned it on his breast as he lay in the coffin.

As the years passed, the Curé continued to spend himself for the souls who sought him out; praying, preaching, solving delicate problems of conscience through a supernatural intuition or wisdom – he had no time to study or prepare, yet always gave the precise advice needed.

In 1859 he became very ill; he told his parishioners that he would die within three weeks. This was the 15th of July. He still went to the church without fail at one o'clock in the morning. Then, on the 29th of July, he was unable to stay in the Confessional, fainting several times. He tried to preach, weeping, but at last allowed himself to be taken to his room where a mattress had been placed on his wooden bed. He received the last Sacraments with great devotion and died peacefully on the 4th of August at 2.00 a.m. whilst one of the priests attending him was reading the prayer for the departing soul: *May the holy angels of God come to meet him and lead him through into the heavenly city...* He was beatified by St Pius X in 1905 and canonized in 1925 by Pius XI. In the encyclical for the centenary of his death Pope John XXIII singled him out as the greatest model of priestly holiness.

SAINT JOHN NEUMANN

Life in Czechoslovakia

In his short autobiography, written in obedience to his religious superior, Saint John Neumann gives some interesting details of his childhood in Czechoslovakia, of his years as a student there and, finally, of his priestly apostolate in America up to the time of his episcopal ordination.

He was the third of six children, two boys and four girls, and was named after John Nepomucene, the saintly patron of Bohemia. As was the custom of practising Catholics, he was baptized the day he was born in 1811, in the church of Saint James, Prachatitz. Agnes, his mother, went to daily Mass, taking one of the children with her. Saint John admits that he often had to be *bribed* to go along, and recalls with amusement that when the mother of one of his young friends held him up as an example to her son, the latter replied, *Give me a penny every day and I'll be like him!*

The memories of his childhood are happy; he enjoyed attending the village school, where he always obtained good marks. Again, in his good-humoured way, he modestly comments that perhaps the fact that his father always held some official position in the town might have had something to do with it. He was in fact very intelligent. From his father he inherited a passionate love of reading. He recalls that he made his first Confession at seven and was confirmed at eight – his memory of this is very clear, as it was the first time anyone could remember a Bishop visiting the town; no doubt this is why the event was celebrated with unusual splendour. Children were not normally allowed to make their first Holy Communion until their early teens, but John was permitted to do so when only nine, all the other first communicants being older. After that, he said, they all went every three months. Not until the pontificate of Saint Pius X did the privilege of receiving Our Lord frequently, and at an early age, become possible. His mother cherished the hope that one day this son of hers would have a vocation to the priesthood, and often reminded him of a comment made by an elderly servant working in the house, that *our little John is going to be a priest*. John himself always considered the priesthood as so exalted a calling as to be beyond his reach, but the thought of its possibility kept recurring and when Latin classes were made available during his schooldays his parents agreed that he should enroll.

The memories of his college days in Budweis are not particularly happy ones. The standard of the college was much lower than expected. More advanced students still had to start in the lowest classes and therefore felt they were wasting their time; it was hardly surprising that they became thoroughly bored. John tells how he took to reading indiscriminately to fill in the idle hours. Little effort seems to have been made to find interesting methods of conveying information to the students, many of whom dropped out of the course. The religious classes were, for John, boring in the extreme – clearly the fault of the teacher – a fact that might account for his great concern for the need of good doctrinal instruction for all his people when he was a priest, and later when he became a bishop.

The two years at the Institute of Philosophy under the Cistercians were a considerable improvement. He now discovered an enthusiasm for many of the subjects he had previously disliked. The change was due mainly to the attitude of the monks, men of prayer who were truly dedicated to the apostolate of teaching. In these final years John had started to attend daily Mass; most of his companions followed his example. At the end of his studies he was torn between going to Prague to study medicine (which his father encouraged) and requesting a place in the Budweis theology seminary – which turned out to have eighty applicants for only twenty places. At the insistence of his mother, John nevertheless sent in his application which, rather to his surprise, was accepted.

In 1831 he began his study of theology in which he made good progress; he appreciated the qualities of the lecturers, but he was quick to notice that the ideas of the professor of Church History were not entirely orthodox. During his second year his interest was aroused in the apostolic field that lay open in America, and in the needs of the German-speaking Catholics who had settled there. Whilst John's first language was Czech, he was fluent in German. Together with another student, Adalbert Schmidt, who was similarly attracted to missionary work, he requested a transfer to the Prague seminary in the hope of learning French and English, which both of them felt would be indispensable if they were to be effective in the apostolate they had in mind.

Prague proved to be a great disappointment. John, brought up in a good Catholic family, had been given sound teaching on the doctrine of the Church from his earliest years. He was angered and saddened to find that several of the professors in the seminary held views clearly opposed to Catholic teaching. Some called into question the authority of the Pope, being influenced by the erroneous claims of the Austrian Emperor Josef II regarding the subordination of the

Church to the State, making the Church merely a State department. The State had passed laws interfering in matters such as Church discipline, cult, etc. and tried to maintain a *national* Church independent of papal authority. John knew how to draw good from evil; this type of error spurred him on to investigate the writings of the Fathers of the Church and those of Saint Thomas Aquinas, Saint Peter Canisius, Saint Robert Bellarmine as well as the Documents of the Council of Trent referring to the Church and the Papacy. One of the theses he produced is a thoroughly orthodox piece of work on papal infallibility (which had not then been defined). Some of his companions ridiculed him for what they considered his *hyper-orthodoxy*, but John continued to be faithful to the authentic teaching of the Church, being well aware that being excessively orthodox is as absurdly impossible as being *slightly orthodox*.

Hopes and disappointments

His hopes of learning English and French were also dashed – the seminarians were told by the Archbishop not to attend the French lectures, and English was not even on the curriculum. On his return to Budweis he found that there were to be no ordinations the year he finished Theology, as the diocese had no need for more priests. The possibility then arose for John and his friend Adalbert to travel to Philadelphia and be ordained by the Archbishop there. Plans again did not work out as expected. The organization which would normally have provided funds refused to do so when requested by the two seminarians. They were told that it was the Archbishop in America who should have made the request if he wanted them. Local parishes came to their aid, but collected only enough for one fare. It was decided that John should go. He went to inform his family, knowing the risk he was taking by going without first having been ordained in case no Bishop in America would accept him, and being well aware also that it could be the last time he would see his family. This last thought made him suffer very much, but he was ready to do whatever God wanted of him, even if it meant this sacrifice. His father agreed very reluctantly, his mother being less upset than her husband. John then made a pilgrimage to the shrine of his patron Saint in Nepomuc, and on the 8th of February 1836 left home without a formal leave-taking – which both he and his family preferred.

More bad news followed – the money for his travelling expenses had already been given to some other missionaries, but for him no other financial assistance was forthcoming. John prayed and persevered in seeking other ways of reaching his destination. After various setbacks he eventually found a ship's captain in Le Havre who was willing to take him to New York for a very reduced fare if he provided his own food. In addition to his few belongings, which included a large box of books, he took along a straw mattress, some potatoes, oil, ham and biscuits and some cooking utensils.

They set sail from France on the 20th of April and they sighted his new country at the end of May after an exhausting journey. He got ashore in New York at the beginning of June. Tired, but glad to be there, and with only one dollar left in his pocket, he set out to find the Bishop, a quest which took him until the next day, walking the streets in the pouring rain, doing his best to ask for directions. Bishop Dubois was very happy to receive the prospective priest, who, not knowing whether his Lordship would be willing to accept him as a candidate for ordination, humbly asked for the loan of his fare to Canada to work among the Indians. In reply, Bishop Dubois smiled, saying he would lend him enough to get to Buffalo, to work there as a priest of the diocese of New York! John remained as a delighted guest of the Bishop until his ordination on the 25th of June. He had been helping to prepare a group of German children for their first Holy Communion and had the joy of giving Our Lord to them for the first time when he celebrated High Mass on Sunday, the 26th of June, the day after Bishop Dubois ordained him.

Soon after his ordination he set off for Buffalo, where he was given the responsibility of caring for the spiritual needs of the German communities scattered throughout several parishes. The children in particular were overjoyed to find a priest who spoke their own language. John quickly realized the need for schools for these youngsters – many spoke neither German nor English correctly. In one place he had to be the school-teacher himself for several months, as the previous one had had to be dismissed and the parishioners could not afford to pay another. John managed to survive on very little. He found accommodation with one of the families until the people built him a small log cabin, which gave him much-needed independence, but with the disadvantage that it entailed a walk of almost two miles through muddy tracks to the nearest church. In 1839 a very welcome visitor arrived in the person of Wenceslaus, his younger brother, who helped him by teaching in the schools John had set up and attending to the household duties.

A Redemptorist

On his journey from New York to Buffalo John had met a Fr Prost, of the Congregation of the Most Holy Redeemer. Later Fr Prost accompanied Bishop Dubois on his visit to the Buffalo area of the diocese.

Fr Prost spoke to Fr John Neumann of the possibility of his having a vocation as a Redemptorist, but the latter did not think that was for him. Shortly afterwards he was asked to help in the parish of Rochester, where Fr Prost had been working. He was amazed at the piety of the people – their frequent reception of the Sacrament of Penance, the devotion they showed in visiting the Blessed Sacrament, all obviously stemming from the doctrinal formation given them by Fr Prost. Fr Neumann wrote to his friend, telling him that he would like to achieve the same results among his own parishioners. The answer made him think. Fr Prost told him the transformation was due to his belonging to the Redemptorists, ending his letter with the words *Vae soli!* (Woe to him who is alone).

After recovering from a quite serious illness early in the year, Fr Neumann wrote on the 4th of September 1840 asking to be admitted into the Congregation of the Most Holy Redeemer, seeing this now as God's will for him. He received an affirmative reply dated the 16th of September. He quickly made the necessary arrangements to travel to Pittsburg, while his brother Wenceslaus gathered his possessions together for him. The boat part of the journey was very bad. It was terrible weather; the remainder, by stage coach, was somewhat better. It took ten days altogether. On the 19th of November he received the Redemptorist habit.

The religious were very few considering the amount of work they had to cover, so Fr Neumann found himself moving from place to place, lending a hand in whatever was necessary. He was always calm and good-humoured, glad to do whatever he could for the good of souls. Rumours that the Congregation was to be dissolved in America caused him great distress and gave rise to doubts as to whether he should not leave and return to work as a diocesan priest. Having prayed earnestly, he saw this as a temptation and remained firm in his vocation. He made his religious profession on the 16th of January 1842, the first Redemptorist to do so in America. He was then transferred to Baltimore, where he began to visit the numerous German families there, some of whom were in danger of losing their faith or of becoming lukewarm in their practice of it.

The sick were of special concern to him, and several hours of each day were soon occupied with instructing prospective converts. He continued to work for schools which would foster the faith of the children, following up the task begun by their parents. In 1847 he was appointed Superior of the Redemptorists in America, a very demanding responsibility. His mother died in 1849, but because of the difficulty in sending and receiving mail he did not hear of her death until two years later. Then he, with the remaining brothers and sisters, left all the family property to their father during his lifetime; at his death it was all to be given for use as a hospital run by religious in Prachatitz.

Care of a diocese

In 1851 Fr Neumann was appointed Bishop by Pope Pius IX. The proposal had been put forward by his friend Archbishop Kenrick of Baltimore. Knowing the humility of Fr Neumann he had informed the Pope that he would probably refuse the honour, so when the papal document arrived it contained a clause indicating that Fr Neumann should accept without appeal. Fr John's autobiography narrates the event very briefly and ends with the words, *But You, O God, have mercy on us. Thanks be to God and to Mary. Passio Christi conforta me.* (Passion of Christ, strengthen me) – this last prayer being the words he took as the motto for his episcopate.

When Archbishop Kenrick called to deliver the papal bull to Fr Neumann, he happened to be out, so the Archbishop left his own ring and pectoral cross on his desk. Fr Neumann understood. He was ordained bishop on the 28th of March, which was also his forty-first birthday. His diocese was very extensive, some thirty-five thousand square miles, yet he visited each parish every two years, preaching, checking on the schools, perusing the parish registers and administering the Sacraments. He always examined the children before Confirmation, and if he found that someone was insufficiently instructed he used to give the necessary additional teaching himself, and only then confirm the child. He once travelled twenty-five miles across country to confirm one child, a vivid illustration of how he valued this Sacrament, and a lesson which his priests and people would not easily forget. He remained for several days in each place, gave a retreat and heard Confessions. The people felt that their Bishop was truly their Good Shepherd.

One of his first priorities was to ensure that Catholics would have a good working knowledge of their faith. Parents, priests and teachers were all exhorted and encouraged by Bishop Neumann to take an active part in transmitting the doctrine of the Church to those under their care. From his early days as a priest he had shown by his own example how vitally important he considered this duty to be. The churches were very few for such a large area, ninety-two in all, with only just over a hundred diocesan priests. There were also a few religious orders who ran educational or other charitable institutions. The seminary at that time had forty-three candidates for the priesthood. The Catholic population was widely scattered, some living in remote outlying districts, miles away from each other. Nor was distance the only problem to be faced.

Catholic immigrants had come from various European countries and a high proportion of them could not speak English. Bishop Neumann during his pastoral work as a priest had, in addition to his native Czech and German, learned French, English, Italian and Spanish in order to help his people. Hours of his time during the pastoral visits were spent in hearing Confessions; those who felt unable to manage in English were overjoyed to be able to make themselves understood in their own language. He even learned sufficient Gaelic to attend to those who had arrived from Western Ireland. He must have been amused and gratified by the ecstatic exclamation of one good lady as she left the confessional, *Thanks be to God that we have an Irish Bishop!* On his travels he took with him a portable altar so that Mass could be said for those who were too far away from a Catholic church. As the Eucharistic fast was then from midnight, he frequently had nothing to eat until after mid-day in his concern that his people should be able to assist at the Holy Sacrifice.

Piety and formation

He always insisted that everything in any way connected with the liturgy, and especially with the Blessed Sacrament, should be kept spotlessly clean and be the best that circumstances would permit. The ceremonies were to be celebrated with all possible dignity and reverence, faithfully adhering to the indications given in the rubrics. In order to promote deeper devotion to Our Lord in the Blessed Sacrament he organized the

Forty Hours devotion at diocesan level soon after his episcopal appointment. Each parish took its turn to have Solemn Exposition for the forty consecutive hours, so that the adoration was continued throughout the diocese during the year. To foster the life of piety and the religious formation of the people he introduced a variety of associations and confraternities, such as that of the Blessed Sacrament (which he instituted himself), the Rosary, the Scapular and the Society of Saint Vincent de Paul for the relief of those in need. Parishioners were helped to follow the liturgical seasons by means, for example, of the Lenten devotions and the Way of the Cross with a sermon and Benediction. He was to be found among the other Redemptorists who gave missions in various churches.

A new religious congregation owed its origin to him; they were the Sisters of the Third Order of Saint Francis Xavier. When in Rome for his *ad limina* visit in 1854, Bishop Neumann told Pope Pius IX of his concern for the children of immigrants left orphans and who, if adopted by non-Catholic families, would be in danger of losing their faith, and told him how badly needed were persons trained to give Catholic education through the schools. The Pope suggested he should found a religious congregation for these purposes and by the following year the first vocations came. The Bishop, like the Pope, believed very firmly that the salvation and sanctity of the people depended to a great extent on the holiness of their priests. He organized, and on occasion gave, retreats for them each year and held theological conferences in various areas several times annually for them to keep up to date in their doctrinal and pastoral formation. His fatherly concern for his priests caused him to set up a society in which priests committed themselves to offer two Masses when they heard of the death of one of their fellow priests.

The visit to Rome coincided with the solemn declaration on the 8th of December of the Dogma of the Immaculate Conception of the Blessed Virgin Mary. Two of his early pastoral letters to the diocese were concerned with Our Lady and the privilege of her Immaculate Conception. To celebrate the dogmatic proclamation he organized a triduum in her honour and was deeply moved by the devotion shown by the crowds who attended.

As the number of Catholics was constantly growing, so too was the need for priests. The few who came to help from Europe were not enough; he needed vocations from among the people of his own diocese – more especially, perhaps, from those whose native tongue was other than English. He started a junior seminary, and this, together with increased numbers in the major seminary, provided a constant source of well-instructed and devout priests for the future. Vocations to his own Congregation also multiplied. Wenceslaus, his brother, was one of these; and later, to their great joy, their nephew John Bayar also became a Redemptorist and was ordained in 1865.

His aim of setting up a school in each parish and the need to find funds for the completion of the Cathedral in Philadelphia, whose building had been initiated by his predecessor, was a heavy burden on top of all his pastoral work. He requested that the diocese be divided and a second Bishop appointed; the decision taken, however, was to nominate an auxiliary Bishop to assist him with his duties in his own diocese.

He always gave himself unstintingly whenever the salvation of a soul was at stake, more especially when the task was seemingly hopeless. His visits to two brothers condemned for murder bore the fruit for which he had prayed and offered penances. Both were reconciled to the Church, receiving the Sacraments before their execution. As he saw so clearly that Christ's death was the price paid for every soul, he would never give anyone up as lost.

By 1860 there were clear signs that his health had been undermined by his demanding pace of life. In the afternoon of the 5th of January, although feeling unwell, he set out on several errands, commenting to another priest that the fresh air would do him good. He also said that one had always to be ready for death, as it would come when and how God willed. He collapsed in the street on his way home and was taken to a house nearby. The family immediately sent for a priest, who anointed him, and a doctor who did his best to save him. When his body was taken back to the Bishop's residence, it was discovered that one of his penances had been to wear a spiked metal cilice. Saint John knew that if he, the Bishop, did not practice penance, it would be unlikely that anybody in his flock would do so! The news of his death reached the whole diocese very quickly, being announced at all the Masses on the following day, the feast of the Epiphany.

Arrangements were made for the body of the Bishop to lie in his own church throughout the day, the lying-in-state being followed by the funeral in the evening. The Redemptorists, however, in accordance with a wish he had expressed, asked for him to be buried in their church, Saint Peter's. Enormous crowds filled both churches, with thousands more lining the route between the two. The people reverently expressed their respect and love, many of them touching the body with rosaries or other items to be kept as relics of their beloved Bishop, whom they already considered a saint.

As time passed, more and more came to pray by

his tomb, asking for favours, both spiritual and material, through his intercession. The list of miracles increased rapidly. The process of his cause for beatification and canonization was opened by Pope Leo XIII in 1896 – the first time this had taken place for an American citizen. When in 1921 Pope Benedict XV issued the decree stating that John Neumann had lived the theological and other virtues to an heroic degree, he stated that heroism in virtue does not mean doing something extraordinary, but rather consisted in fulfilling the normal duties of one's state faithfully; in other words he was reiterating the truth that sanctity is attainable for all, whatever their position in life, if they make use of the graces God gives them. Saint John was canonized in 1977 by Pope Paul VI on the 19th of June, and his feast is kept on the 5th of January.

BLESSED JOSEMARIA ESCRIVA

"Pray for me that I may be good and faithful to the end" – the parting words of Blessed Josemaría Escrivá in March 1975 to some twenty members of Opus Dei who were leaving Rome after an international university congress. The short, family-type get-together three days before his priestly Golden Jubilee finished with Josemaría Escrivá giving them the blessing for a journey – the journey of life as he put it. Then as a practical way of reminding the travellers of his request for prayers, and a sign of his great love for Our Lady, each received a rosary which he had blessed. For many of those present it was the last time they saw him. Three months later, almost to the day, on the 26th of June 1975 the Father, as he was always referred to by everyone in Opus Dei, reached the end of his journey in this life, having indeed been good and faithful to all that God had asked of him.

Childhood

Josemaría Escrivá was born in Barbastro, Spain, on the 9th of January 1902, the second of six children. At the age of two he became so seriously ill that the doctor informed his parents, José and Dolores Escrivá that there was no hope for their son. They then put all their trust in the intercession of Our Lady, promising her that if their child recovered they would make a pilgrimage to her small country shrine of Torreciudad in the Pyrenees. The following morning the doctor returned to enquire when the baby had died and was amazed to see Josemaría playing happily in his cot. The grateful parents fulfilled their promise, carrying their small son up the stony mountain tracks to the small eleventh century shrine where they offered him to Our Lady.

Thanks to the example and teaching of their parents Christian piety was a normal part of life for the children. They taught them to make a simple morning offering, accompanied them to Sunday Mass and said the rosary together each day. Josemaría's sister Carmen was two years his senior, and after him came three more girls – María Asunción, María Dolores and Rosario – and finally another boy, Santiago, who was born when Josemaría was seventeen. The family were very united; the children saw and grew to imitate the affection, serenity and concern for others shown by Mr and Mrs Escrivá, and also their love for truth and fortitude in the face of difficulties. Their mother helped to prepare the children for their first Confession and Holy Communion. Josemaría was ten when he received Our Lord for the first time. He always remembered and taught many other people a prayer of preparation: *I wish Lord, to receive you with the purity, humility and devotion with which your most holy Mother received you, with the spirit and fervour of the saints.* In later life Blessed Josemaría would say this very frequently, when making a visit to Our Lord in the Blessed Sacrament and at other times in the day.

Experience of the Cross

The bond between the parents and their two elder children – Carmen and Josemaría – was deepened by their grief when, within three years, first Rosario the baby died; then, two years later, María Dolores when she was five, and in 1913 María Asunción the eight-year old. The parents gently explained to the disconsolate children that their little sisters were happy in Heaven for ever. The serene and loving acceptance of God's will, even though it cost his parents so much, was a lesson Josemaría never forgot.

Sorrow of a different kind came some time later when the family business ran into serious difficulties due to mismanagement by one of the partners. Because of his Christian sense of honesty, Mr Escrivá ensured that payment was made to all the creditors although legally this was not strictly necessary. As a result the family were impoverished and Mr Escrivá had to seek other employment. He moved with the family to Logroño where he patiently started again. Josemaría continued his studies there and soon made new friends, among them Isidoro Zorzano, a fellow-student, whose parents had lived for some years in Argentina where Isidoro was born.

Seeking God's Will

"Already in adolescence Josemaría perceived God's call to a life of greater commitment" (John Paul II, Beatification Homily, 17 May 1992). The turning point came in Josemaría's life one cold winter morning in 1917-18 around his sixteenth birthday. Walking along the street through the snow he saw in front of him the prints left by the feet of a discalced Carmelite. The impression caused by the evidence of what the holy man was ready to do for the love of God made Josemaría reflect. He then began to attend Mass and receive Holy Communion daily and to go to Confession frequently, praying to see what God was asking of him. He saw that in order to be totally available for whatever was God's Will, he should become a priest. This entailed a complete change in his plans and those of his father. Josemaría felt this very keenly when he decided to speak to him – it was the first and only time he had seen his father cry. The advice the boy received was to think it over very carefully … to realize that a priest had to be a saint … that it would be very hard not to have a home or a love on earth. But he promised not to oppose his son's decision, and introduced him to a priest friend who could help. When the arrangements were made for him to go to the seminary, Josemaría, his parents' only son, prayed that God would send them another to take his place. In 1919 his brother Santiago was born. As a seminarian in Logroño and Saragossa, Josemaría often repeated the petition of Bartimaeus, the blind man of Jericho, *Lord, that I may see!* (Luke 19:41) – a prayer he was to continue for several years.

The day of his ordination came on the 28th of March 1925, the joy again accompanied by the Cross; his father had died suddenly four months before. The first Mass that Josemaría offered was for his father. His first appointment was to the small village of Perdiguera where, in addition to his daily Mass, he held Exposition of the Blessed Sacrament, fostering a deep devotion to the Holy Eucharist among his parishioners. On his return to Saragossa he often went to the basilica of El Pilar, praying continuously *to see* what God wanted. He had finished his degree in Law in Saragossa, and in 1927 the Bishop allowed him to move to Madrid where he did his doctorate. He also gave classes in Canon Law and Roman Law to help support himself, his mother, Carmen and Santiago. He became chaplain to the Foundation for the Sick which cared for poor people who were ill, visiting them in their homes. Fr Escrivá celebrated Mass, administered the Sacraments and prepared the children for their first Holy Communion, as many as four thousand in one year. He was very concerned that none of those who was sick should die without the Sacraments, and gave himself unstintingly, covering considerable distances on foot to reach them.

The answer to prayer

On the feast of the Guardian Angels, the 2nd of October 1928, Fr Escrivá was making a retreat when he saw very clearly the answer he had been praying for. It came just when the bells of the nearby church of Our Lady of the Angels began to ring. The work he was being asked to undertake – this Work of God, Opus Dei – was to show ordinary Christians how they could sanctify their lives in the midst of their normal everyday work and activities, dedicating these to God, helping their families, friends and colleagues to get to know and love God. The young priest, only twenty-six years old, felt that he had nothing – except as he put it, the grace of God and a good sense of humour – to begin this great supernatural task. But, "with supernatural intuition, Blessed Josemaría untiringly preached the universal call to holiness and the apostolate" (John Paul II, Beatification Homily, 17 May 1992). As always he relied on the power of prayer, his own and that of others, especially of the sick and the dying whom he attended in the hospitals and poor areas of the city. Little by little he was joined by a few young men, mainly students, to whom he gave spiritual formation, teaching them to pray, to offer their study or work – which had to be well done – and to deepen in their knowledge of the truths of the Faith in order to have a solid, doctrinal life of piety, enabling them to be apostles among their contemporaries.

1930 brought a further development. On the 14th of February while saying Mass, Fr Escrivá saw that women would also form part of this Work of God. The apostolic panorama seemed almost infinite. How many souls in all walks of life would be able to put themselves at the service of God, through a divine vocation, bringing Christ into their environments as did the early Christians! The burden of Fr Escrivá's work was increased by the need to give formation to the members of the Work, one of whom was his Argentinian friend Isidoro. As his mother's home had become too small for the groups of students coming for classes, Fr Escrivá found a flat which could serve as an academy.

The Spanish civil war

Growing unrest and anti-Catholic feeling in Spain finally came to a head in 1936 with the outbreak of the civil war. Many churches and convents were destroyed by fires, thousands of priests and religious were murdered. The new republican government issued orders closing churches, forbidding all acts of cult and expropriating the buildings of monasteries, convents and charitable institutions. Search parties entered private houses without warning; nowhere was safe for a priest. Fr Escrivá took refuge for short periods in various places, continuing his pastoral work, keeping in contact as far as possible with the young people of the Work. As the difficulties of avoiding arrest increased, the others convinced him to try to escape to the nationalist zone, which involved reaching Barcelona and from there crossing the Pyrenees into Andorra and thence to France, and back again into Spain to Burgos which was under nationalist control. The journey through the Pyrenees was extremely hazardous. The group which included several members of the Work was quite numerous; they had to hide during the day and travel by night in the bitter cold of November, hungry and exhausted, with the constant danger of being caught and shot by the republican garrisons. Eventually the weary group of men crossed safely into Andorra and made their way over the French border. Fr Escrivá's first stop with his companions was in Lourdes where he offered Mass in thanksgiving.

He resumed his apostolic activities in and around Burgos and re-entered Madrid at the first opportunity at the end of the war. His visit to the students' residence which had replaced the earlier academy revealed only a heap of rubble – the only item still intact was a card which had been on the wall of the study room with the words from Saint John's Gospel (15:12) *Mandatum novum do vobis; ut diligatis invicem sicut dilexi vos.* (This is my commandment, that you should love one another as I have loved you.)

New beginnings and persecution

The work of formation and apostolate continued. Numerous requests also came from bishops for him to preach retreats to priests in many dioceses of Spain. A new residence was started, again with nothing. His mother and sister went to take care of the housekeeping until, in 1941, his mother died unexpectedly while Fr Escrivá was giving a retreat for priests in Lérida. Carmen then continued on her own, achieving a true family atmosphere in the residence by her attention to small details of order, cleanliness and decoration which made the students feel *at home*. Fr Escrivá used to take the more willing students to visit the hospitals with patients from the poorest areas of Madrid, as he had done earlier. Contact with the destitute, the terminally ill and the lonely had a profound effect on the young people – they helped the sufferers through their generosity and spirit of sacrifice, doing whatever they could to alleviate them and they in turn received a tangible example of Christian fortitude and saw the supernatural value of pain.

During the early 1940's criticism and slander were directed against Fr Escrivá and against Opus Dei. The idea that the ordinary faithful were called to a vocation of sanctity (brought out very clearly a quarter of a century later in the teachings of the Second Vatican Council) was considered by some clerics at that time as a heresy.

Some of those who chose to attack Opus Dei went to the length of telling the parents of members of the Work that their children were on the road to perdition. Others stated that the liturgical and eucharistic symbols (the cross, the dove, ears of wheat) used in the decoration of the oratory of one of the Centres were masonic!

All this, which Fr Escrivá referred to as *the persecution of good people*, caused him to suffer very much. His reaction was always to forgive and pray for his detractors, at the same time teaching the members of the Work to do likewise. In the midst of this time of trial God enabled him to see how there could be priests in Opus Dei. He realized that lay members, who had lived the spirit of Opus Dei, needed to be ordained to serve the members of the Work effectively and to cooperate in their apostolates. The first three were ordained on the 25th of June 1944, Fr Alvaro del Portillo, Fr José María Hernández Garnica and Fr José Luis Muzquiz. By 1975 nearly a thousand members of Opus Dei had become priests.

Rome and the expansion of the Work
Approval of Opus Dei had been given in the early days by the Bishop of Madrid, but once peace was restored after World War II, Fr Escrivá knew that

pontifical approval would be necessary for the Work to extend throughout the world. In 1946 Fr del Portillo went to Rome for this purpose. He soon realized that little would be achieved unless the Founder himself went to explain the Work. In the Vatican he had been told that Opus Dei had arrived a century too soon – it did not fit into the existing legal framework. Despite the fact that Fr Escrivá was very ill and had been warned by his doctor not to undertake the journey, he set off from Barcelona in June 1946 after visiting the Basilica of El Pilar in Saragossa, the Monastery of Montserrat and the Basilica of Our Lady of Ransom in Barcelona to ask for the assistance of the Mother of God. Exhausted as he was after the stormy crossing to Genoa and the long drive to Rome, Fr Escrivá remained all the first night in prayer by the window of the small flat in the Piazza della Città Leonina which faced Saint Peter's and the papal apartments in the Vatican. It was a way of giving expression to his immense love for the Pope, the Vicar of Christ on earth.

Pope Pius XII received Fr Escrivá and approvals were granted by the Holy See. Opus Dei is now a Personal Prelature which was the legal framework in the Church that the Founder had always wanted for the Work. Fr Escrivá returned briefly to Madrid before establishing the central offices of the Work in Rome. In April 1947 he was appointed Domestic Prelate to the Pope, receiving the title of Monsignor. Among the Prelates in the Vatican who showed great interest in and affection for Opus Dei and its Founder was Monsignor Giovanni-Battista Montini, who was later to bear the great burden of the entire Church as Pope Paul VI.

The Work began in new countries, spreading rapidly to all five continents, carrying the same spirit to peoples of all races, nations and cultures, enabling them to *learn to turn all the circumstances and events of their lives into opportunities to love God and to serve the Church, the Pope and all souls with joy and simplicity, lighting up the paths of the earth with faith and love.* In 1946 the Work began in Portugal and England; next came Ireland in 1947 and France the following year, then further afield, to the United States and Mexico in 1949. 1952 saw the beginnings in Germany. Other European and South American countries followed. The Far East (Japan) and the African continent (Kenya) started in 1958; the apostolic work commenced in Australia and the Philippines in the early 1960's and since then it has spread to new countries in Africa and Eastern Europe.

International centres were set up in Rome for the formation of members of the Work, many of whom would travel to new countries to carry on the apostolic work there, bringing many converts into the Church and teaching people from all environments to deepen in their Christian life. In the decree of the Holy See of the 9th of April, 1990, Josemaría was recognized as *a real pioneer of the intrinsic unity of Christian life, proclaiming the fullness of a contemplative life 'in the middle of the street' and calling all the faithful to take an active part in the apostolates of the Church from the place each one occupies in the world.*

Corporate undertakings

Blessed Josemaría had often encouraged those who joined Opus Dei in the early years to broaden their horizons, asking them "to dream and your dreams will fall short". In addition to the personal apostolate of each individual member, the variety of corporate works of Opus Dei, many of which the Founder inspired during his lifetime, continues to increase. These are undertakings initiated by members of Opus Dei with friends and colleagues not in Opus Dei. Their purpose is always spiritual and apostolic, a service to society, never commercial.

These corporate works range from clubs for young people, residences for young workers or students to schools, universities, dispensaries, training establishments for workers and conference centres. At each one, the civil body responsible for the establishment has asked the Opus Dei Prelature to be responsible for the doctrinal and pastoral care offered there. Activities are open to all who wish to benefit, whatever their creed, social status or ethnic background.

Over the years, hundreds of thousands of people from all walks of life have benefited from the cultural, professional and doctrinal formation imparted in one or other of these corporate works. They have learned to live and work in an atmosphere of mutual respect, understanding and friendship with others, whose viewpoints might be very different from their own. For some, contact with the club, residence or training centre, as been their first encounter with Christianity; others have discovered the way to give a Christian focus to their professional and family life.

One corporate work, perhaps an exception in the way it was born, is Centro ELIS (Educazione, Lavoro, Istruzione, Sport) in the industrial Tiburtino district of Rome, where communism is rife. It began when Pope John XXIII asked Opus Dei to take charge of a social project funded by donations which had been raised for the eightieth birthday of Pope Pius XII. When Pope Paul VI opened the completed project in 1965, he was accompanied by Blessed Josemaría. The Centre comprises of two technical training Colleges and a residence for over a hundred young people, from Italy and from overseas; the adjacent parish church is attended to by priests of the Prelature. In 1984 Pope John Paul II visited ELIS.

The corporate works, which are not profit-making enterprises, are financed partly by the fees paid by those who attend them. Members, friends and Co-operators of Opus Dei help with donations and fund-raising, in appreciation of the apostolic work carried out and the social welfare and educational facilities which are imbued with a Christian spirit of service.

Apostolic journeys

Blessed Josemaría visited most of the countries of Europe to prepare the future work there or to give guidance and encouragement to members of Opus Dei already living there. On some occasions, as in Spain in 1972 and in Central and South America in the following years, thousands of people, the majority of whom were not in Opus Dei, went to listen to Monsignor Escrivá. Although the people were so numerous at these gatherings there was still a family atmosphere. Blessed Josemaría spoke of what was in his heart – the love of God, the Christian virtues which all the faithful are called to practise, the possibility and challenge for each one to give his or her entire life to God's service there in the fulfilment of their family, social and professional duties. *The merit of his contribution to the promotion of the laity is to be found in this Christianization of the world from within* (Decree, 9th of April 1990).

He had a remarkable talent for expressing his message – Christ's message – in words suited to his hearers, whether they were busy mothers of families, people with little culture, doctors, young children or the sick. For the latter he had a special affection, telling them to see suffering as a share in the Passion of Jesus Christ. By uniting themselves to His sacrifice they could be marvellous instruments helping in Christ's work of Redemption. Children (and their parents) were delighted when he told them that their best friends were their mother and father, that they should go to them with all their worries and questions. He reminded parents to win their children's confidence, to make time to listen to them, to spend time with them, to be understanding and at the same time teaching them to live as good Christians, mainly through their own example.

The theme of the sanctity and dignity of marriage was a frequent topic of his teaching. Married couples were exhorted not to be afraid of having children – each child was a sign of God's confidence in them, entrusting this tender soul to their care, so that they could help form their child in preparation for eternal life. Blessed Josemaría expressed his appreciation of work in the home, explaining to those whose task this was that Mary Immaculate, the Mother of God, spent her life on earth as a housewife and mother, putting all her love into serving the Holy Family in this way, she who is *Daughter of God the Father, Mother of God the Son, Spouse of God the Holy Spirit – greater than you, none but God!* (*The Way*, 496)

Jesus, Mary, the Pope

Blessed Josemaría's words to others were the consequence of his own intense union with God and penetration into the sublime mysteries of the Faith. He often spoke of love for the sacred Humanity of Christ as the way to grow in knowledge for God the Father and God the Holy Spirit. He urged people to get to know Christ through daily reading of the Gospels,

personal prayer and especially through devout attendance at the Sacrifice of the Mass and reception of
Holy Communion. His devotion and desires for making
reparation to Jesus in the Blessed Sacrament were
manifested in many ways: insisting that only the best
should be offered to God as a sign of love and faith,
paying great attention to the dignity of liturgical worship and the cleanliness of everything related to use in
churches and oratories, and his reminder in *The Way*:
When you approach the tabernacle remember that he has
been awaiting you for twenty centuries, (537) and again
There he is King of kings and Lord of lords, hidden in
the Bread. To this extreme he has humbled himself
through love for you (538). The day for Josemaría was
divided into two – the first part for giving thanks for
the Mass and Communion of that morning, the rest a
preparation for that of the following day. His intense
work, his contact with those around him, with visitors
… far from being a distraction was a means of achieving this constant awareness of God's presence and of
bringing those souls nearer to God.

"He likewise has a filial love for the Virgin Mary
which leads him to imitate her virtues" (John Paul II,
Beatification Homily, 17 May 1992). The rosary was
one of his favourite prayers to pay honour and respect
to the Mother of God. His book, *The Holy Rosary*, con-
tains brief considerations on each of the fifteen mysteries. During the course of numerous gatherings he
would remind those present that none of the traditional
devotions of the Church are 'out of date'. Starting from
the pilgrimage to Torreciudad as a child he made many
visits to shrines and churches in honour of the Blessed
Virgin, especially in May, to seek her help and make up
in so far as he could for the neglect and lack of love
shown to her in many places. One of his last *follies*, as

he put it, was the restoration of the shrine of Torreciudad and the construction of a beautiful church in
that remote part of the Pyrenees which is now frequented by thousands of pilgrims every year to honour
Our Lady.

His veneration for the holy Patriarch Saint Joseph
was well-known. When Pope John XXIII included the
name of Saint Joseph in the Roman Canon of the
Mass, one of the Prelates in the Vatican congratulated
Monsignor Escrivá, knowing how happy he would be at
the news. When seeking permission in 1935 for the
first oratory with the Blessed Sacrament in the recently
opened students' residence, he placed this intention in
the hands of Saint Joseph. The request was granted
quickly, and to show his gratitude, Blessed Josemaría
disposed that the tabernacle key of every Centre of the
Work should have attached by a small chain, a medal of
Saint Joseph with the inscription *Ite ad Joseph* (Go to
Joseph).

From the day when Opus Dei came into being
Josemaría was firmly convinced that its purpose was to
serve the Church as the Church wishes to be served.
He always prayed and made others pray, for the person
and intentions of the Holy Father, begging his sons and
daughters in Opus Dei not to allow the Pope to be
alone in carrying the weight of the Church. His fidelity
and loyalty to the Magisterium of the Church was
immovable and outspoken. By his insistence on the
sound formation of the members of the Work he
ensured that they, and those in contact with Opus Dei,
would always obey and uphold the teachings of the
Church in the face of any opposition. He suffered deeply when the disloyalty of some members of the Church
became apparent and doctrinal confusion, with the consequent harm to souls, began to increase. His response

was to intensify his prayer and mortification for the Church and to offer his life that the time of trial should soon come to an end.

Another measure that Blessed Josemaría proposed as a solution to the problems within the Church and in society was for Catholics to have recourse to the true remedy for evil – the Sacrament of Penance. Reiterating the constant teaching of the Popes he encouraged the faithful to receive the sacramental absolution regularly and often – he made his own confession faithfully each week. He spoke of how those who perhaps do not respond to the thought of the greatness of God who is our Creator are moved by the notion of the God who forgives. With graphic examples Josemaría showed the great benefits of this Sacrament, stressing the fact that the priest gives the absolution *in nomine et in persona Christi* (in the name and in the person of Christ). His comparison of a human tribunal, where the judge always inflicts a punishment on the defendant who confesses his guilt, with the divine tribunal of Penance, where Christ is the Judge who always forgives us when we confess our sins with true sorrow, moved many souls to make use of the opportunity to receive this Sacrament and to continue to approach it with greater frequency in the future.

Life is changed, not taken away

Josemaría's awareness of the fact that through Baptism we are indeed children of God permeated the whole of his interior life. From the early 1930's when he was painfully conscious of his incapacity to carry out the supernatural work entrusted to him, a special grace enabled him to perceive the Fatherhood of God and to abandon himself totally to the divine Will with joy and serenity. This sense of divine filiation was to be a characteristic of the spirit of Opus Dei. Among his considerations on the Passion of Our Lord, Blessed Josemaría wrote in his *Way of the Cross: ... Take refuge in your divine sonship: God is your most loving Father. In this lies your security, a haven where you can drop anchor no matter what is happening on the surface of the sea of life. And you will find joy, strength, optimism, victory!* (Seventh Station, no. 2).

Good Friday of the Holy Year 1975 was the fiftieth anniversary of his ordination. Giving thanks for all the graces he had received, he told Our Lord: *"You are what you are – perfect goodness. And I am what I am – the filthiest rag in this rotten world. And yet, you look at me ... and you seek me ... and you love me ... Lord, may I seek you, look at you, love you!"* For some months one of his frequent aspirations had been, *Vultum tuum, Domine, requiram!* (Lord, I seek your face!) He had reminded his sons and daughters in the Work that, having received their vocation from God during the lifetime of their Founder, they were co-founders with the responsibility of continuing the Work, of transmitting the spirit in its entirety to those who would come after them. No one however, realized how soon his move to *our home in Heaven* was to be.

On the 26th of June 1975 Josemaría Escrivá travelled to an international centre for women of Opus Dei, in Castelgandolfo. He asked them to pray very much for the Church and the Pope and for those members of Opus Dei who were going to be ordained in July. The meeting finished sooner than expected, as Josemaría began to feel unwell. After a short rest he returned to Rome with Fr Alvaro del Portillo and Fr Javier Echevarría who had accompanied him. On entering the house, he went immediately, as was his custom, to greet Our Lord in the Blessed Sacrament, and then up to the office where he worked. He went in, glanced with affection at the picture of Our Lady on the wall, and fell to the floor. The heart attack was fatal. Fr del Portillo gave him absolution and the sacrament of the Anointing of the Sick.

An enormous congregation filled the church of San Eugenio at the Solemn Requiem Mass, which was attended by a representative of Pope Paul VI, several cardinals, bishops and ambassadors.

News of the death of the Founder of the Work spread rapidly, and almost as rapidly, letters began to pour into Rome requesting the initiation of his cause of canonisation. As time passed more and more testimonies arrived of favours received, both spiritual and material, through his intercession. The chapel in Viale Bruno Buozzi 75 in Rome, where the body of Josemaría Escrivá was laid to rest was visited by more and more people every day; some to seek his intercession, others to give thanks. The decree introducing the cause for beatification and canonisation was promulgated in 1981, and in May of that year, two processes began, in Rome and Madrid, to study his life and virtues. In 1982 and 1983 two further processes started for the examination of extraordinary cures attributed to Josemaría. In April 1990 the Church officially declared that the Founder of Opus Dei had lived the Christian virtues to an heroic degree. On the 6th of July 1991 the Holy Father Pope John Paul II read the decree by which a miraculous cure was recognized as due to Josemaría's intercession. He was beatified on the 17th of May, 1992 in a packed St Peter's Square in Rome, where some 200,000 people had gathered together from every corner of the globe to give thanks to God. The spirit of Opus Dei has reached countless souls through the writings of the Founder; millions of copies have been published of *The Way, Holy Rosary, Furrow, The Forge, The Way of the Cross*, which have all been translated into many languages, as also three collections of homilies; *Christ is passing by*, *Friends of God* and *In Love with the Church*.

His influence on many lives continues. As he had been *good and faithful to the end*, thousands of others too have given their lives to God, seeking to love and serve Our Lord by sanctifying the everyday realities of life. "The relevance and transcendence of this spiritual message, deeply rooted in the Gospel, are evident, as is also shown in the fruitfulness with which God has blessed the life and work of Josemaría Escrivá" (John Paul II, Beatification Homily, 17 May 1992).

SAINT JOSEPH

There is a painting in the National Gallery in London by the famous Spanish artist Bartolomé Estaban Murillo which presents to us graphically the sublime grandeur of Saint Joseph. It is entitled *The Two Trinities*, and depicts the Three Persons of the Blessed Trinity, along with Our Lady and Saint Joseph on either side of the Holy Child. Saint Joseph's life was entirely at the service of God, inseparably linked in a mysterious way to the Blessed Trinity. He, more than any other Saint, was close to Jesus and Mary, chosen as he had been from eternity in the Divine plan to love, protect and provide for the Son of God made man and his Immaculate Mother.

Saint Joseph in the Gospels

The Gospels of Saint Matthew and Saint Luke give us few but vitally important facts about Saint Joseph. Saint Matthew begins his Gospel with a genealogy of Jesus, tracing back his ancestors through David to Abraham, finishing the list with *and Jacob was the father of Joseph, the husband of Mary; it was of her that Jesus was born, who is called Christ*, (Matt 1:1-16). In Saint Luke 3:23-38, we are told that *He (Jesus) was by repute the son of Joseph, son of Heli...* showing his descent again through David, from Adam. Being the husband of Mary the Mother of Jesus, Saint Joseph was considered by Jewish law as having the rights and duties of a father to her son, although not being physically his father; Jesus' belonging to the royal house of David is because of Joseph.

Saint Luke (1:26-27) introduces us to both Our Lady and Saint Joseph: *God sent the Angel Gabriel to a city of Galilee called Nazareth, where a virgin dwelt, betrothed to a man of David's lineage; his name was Joseph and the virgin's name was Mary.* The variations in the two lists of ancestors given by the evangelists can be explained by the Jewish custom of a younger brother marrying the widow of his elder brother who had died childless, in order to raise up children in the elder brother's name. Saint Matthew names Saint Joseph's real father Jacob, whilst Saint Luke gives the name of his legal father, Heli.

From the Gospels – the only source of information – we learn that Saint Joseph was by profession a carpenter, or possibly a blacksmith. (The Greek version calls him τεκτων (*tekton*), which usually meant someone who worked with wood; the Latin *faber* could mean a metal worker). Quite possibly he did both. His income was modest; when the time came for the Child to be presented in the Temple, the offering made by the Holy Family was that of the poor – two doves or young pigeons.

Husband of Mary

Just as God had chosen and prepared Mary to be the virginal Mother of the Word made flesh, so Joseph was destined to be her virginal husband and father, head of the Holy Family. The marriage ceremony in those times consisted of two parts – the first, a private contract which was a true marriage, and some months later, the public wedding when the bride was escorted to her husband's home. On several occasions the Gospels refer to Mary as Joseph's wife (Matt 1:20; Luke 2:5). Theirs was a true marriage, each loving the other with the pure love of a spouse, each preserving their virginity as God's will for them. Both were young at the time of their marriage – Mary probably around fifteen, as was the custom, and Joseph a few years older. Some artists have portrayed Saint Joseph as an old man, with no evidence to support this idea, which does not in any case even fit in with what we know of what Joseph had to undertake. God chose the most perfect of his creatures for the Mother of Jesus; He also chose the man who was to act as his father, nothing less, and be the perfect spouse for Mary.

When the momentous announcement was made to Mary that she was to be the Mother of the long-awaited Messiah by the power of the Holy Spirit, the message for the time being was for her alone.

When Joseph saw that she was with Child, knowing her immaculate purity and holiness he was confronted with a mystery. The word *justus*, used to describe Saint Joseph, signifies justice, uprightness and sanctity. He, like Mary, must have read and pondered upon the writings of the prophets concerning the Messiah, understanding far more than the rest of their people. Perhaps he realized that Isaiah's prediction of the virgin who was to conceive had been fulfilled in Mary and therefore felt himself unworthy to share in the mystery. Whilst loving her so much, he was even willing to offer the sacrifice of separation if that was to be what God wanted of him.

His troubled mind was set at rest very soon: *Hardly had this thought come to his mind when an Angel of the Lord appeared to him in a dream and said, Joseph, son of David, do not be afraid to take thy wife Mary to thyself, for it is by the power of the Holy Spirit that she has conceived this Child; and she will bear a son, whom thou shalt call Jesus, for He is to save his people from their sins.* (Matt 1:20-21). The Angel addressed him by his royal title and revealed his future role: it would be to act as a true father to the Son of God. He it was who would give the Child his name when He came to be circumcised. Mary had also been told this name and its significance. Now she and Joseph could share their joy together.

God's instrument

There is no record of any words spoken by Saint Joseph. He passes almost unnoticed, carrying out his duties, totally obedient to God and to those whom the Creator used as his instruments. Living as they did in Nazareth, Mary and Joseph must have wondered how the prophecy of Micheas 5:2 would be fulfilled, concerning the place from which the leader of Israel was to come. News of the census organized by Augustus, which for many would have been a source of annoyance, filled the hearts of Joseph and Mary with joy. Far away in Rome, Augustus, perhaps the greatest of the emperors, was unaware of how he was co-operating with the designs of the God he did not know. Because of his efficient government and superb military skill, the *pax Augusta* had come into effect. Peace reigned throughout the whole Empire, an appropriate setting for the coming of the Prince of Peace. One of his poets, the great Virgil, had written a poem foretelling a golden age of peace and joy to be ushered in by the birth of a very special child, giving tender descriptions of this child with his mother. The poem was produced as a tribute to Caesar Augustus, but because of its content it has been called the *messianic eclogue*.

Hearing of the census, Joseph proceeded to carry out his civic duty, taking Mary with him to Bethlehem. There for the first time they experienced what the promised Redeemer was to be – a *Man of Sorrows*, rejected by his own people even before He was born. Joseph continued searching diligently until he found a place where Mary could have the privacy she needed. The stable was not wonderful, but was the best Joseph could offer; what mattered was that he offered it with love.

Shortly after the birth of Jesus the family were visited by the group of shepherds, telling them about the message of the Angels and the signs by which they were to recognize the Saviour – particularly the humble surroundings of the manger in the stable.

Saint Luke goes on to describe two more events in which Saint Joseph took part; the rite of circumcision of the Child, signifying the pact made by God with his chosen people, and the Presentation of Jesus in the Temple at Jerusalem (Luke 2:21-39). Joseph must have been profoundly moved by the words of Simeon and Anna, revealing that the Redeemer had come to save the non-Jewish nations, not only the people of Israel. Sorrow again overshadowed joy; Jesus would be rejected and Mary would suffer on his account. Joseph's heart ached for both of them.

Back again in Bethlehem, Saint Matthew narrates the arrival of the three travellers from foreign lands, the Wise Men, gentiles, among those who *seek God with a sincere heart* (Eucharistic prayer IV). Simeon's prophecy! From the evangelist's description, Saint Joseph had already found a house in Bethlehem; the Wise Men *going into the dwelling, found the Child there with his Mother Mary, and fell down to worship him* (Matt 2:11). Joseph heard their account of the wonderful star, of their long journey leading they knew not where, of their absolute confidence in God's guidance. He saw their faith as they prostrated themselves in adoration, their love as they offered their treasures, and he knew the infinite gift he possessed. Saint Bernard wrote of him: *Joseph, blessed and happy man, who wast permitted to see and hear the God whom many kings wished in vain to see and hear; and not only to see and hear him, but carry him in your arms, kiss him, clothe him and care for him – pray for us!*

The Wise Men took their leave and that very same night the Angel again spoke – this time with urgency. *Rise up, take with thee the Child and his Mother and flee to Egypt; there remain until I give thee word, for Herod will soon be making search for the Child to destroy him.* (Matt 2:13). Joseph obeys instantly: *He rose up therefore, while it was still night, and took the child and his Mother with him and withdrew into Egypt* (Matt 2:14). He does not try to rationalize or give his own opinion; like Mary, Joseph was sensitive to the least motion of the Holy Spirit, to the slightest indication of the Will of God. The journey in haste, by night, through desert country, with the constant fear of being overtaken by Herod's troops, was very difficult – and their destination was a pagan land where for centuries the people of Israel had lived in slavery. Joseph would have to find them a house; most of their possessions had been left behind in Bethlehem; they would have to learn a new language; the angel had given no indication as to how long they were to stay – there were so many difficulties. Joseph did not consider these. He thought only that the Child and his Mother were safe, and he was with them. Prompt obedience was what God asked of him, and he was always ready to obey.

Nazareth

After some time he received another brief message from the Angel, following the death of Herod, telling him to return to his own country. From Saint

Matthew we see how Joseph used his initiative to find the best way of obeying, and how he received confirmation of his plan: *When he heard that Archelaus was king in Judaea in the place of his father Herod, he was afraid to return there; and so, receiving a warning in a dream, he withdrew into the region of Galilee, where he came to live in a town called Nazareth* (Matt 2:22-23). Both the sojourn in Egypt and their settling in Nazareth were in fulfilment of the ancient prophecies.

No details are given of the life of the Holy Family during the years spent in Nazareth except for one incident which took place on one of their annual visits to Jerusalem for the great feast of the Passover (Luke 2:41-52). Jesus by now was twelve years old. He stayed behind, and neither Mary nor Joseph realized this until the separate groups of men and women on their way home met when they stopped for the night. As children could go with either group, each thought he was with the other. For three days they searched, retracing their steps all the way back to Jerusalem. Mary already felt her heart pierced by the sword Simeon had spoken of. This was in itself a foreshadowing of that other separation for three days, with his dead body lying in the tomb.

On finding Jesus they were amazed, first at seeing him asking and answering questions among the teachers, and then at realizing that he was not lost as they had imagined. Mary's exclamation shows her deference to her husband as head of the family – *Think what anguish of mind thy father and I have suffered...* The reply of Jesus was for them a mystery too deep to comprehend: *What reason had you to search for me? Could you not tell that I must needs be in the place which belongs to My Father?* These words which he spoke to them were beyond their understanding. The sequel also gives food for meditation. *He went down with them on their journey to Nazareth and lived there in subjection to them* – Jesus, Son of God, Second Person of the Blessed Trinity, All-powerful, All-wise, lived in obscurity, obeying two of his creatures. Saint Joseph and Mary kept in their hearts the memory of all this.

In fulfilling his appointed task as head of the Holy Family in Nazareth, Saint Joseph is a model for everyone. He loved, cared for and conversed with Jesus and Mary with all naturalness about small everyday matters – as we can too. Joseph earned his living, supported his family through ordinary work and taught Jesus his trade. St Joseph 'the Worker' gives a proof of the supernatural value and dignity of every upright human occupation if it is done to the best of one's ability and offered to God. By following his example and asking for his assistance in all aspects of our life, each one of us can come closer to Mary, and through her to Jesus who shows us the way to the Father and the Holy Spirit.

Since there is no mention of Saint Joseph when Jesus starts his public life – he is not present with Mary at the marriage feast at Cana – it is assumed that he was already dead. Saint Joseph, the greatest Saint after Our Lady, lived and died quietly, showing the great value of humility and of the little ordinary details of every-day life in the eyes of God.

Devotion to Saint Joseph

For some years in the early Church there is little evidence of devotion to him, but with the passing of time this devotion has increased enormously. In the fourth century Saint Ephraim said: *No-one can praise Saint Joseph sufficiently*. Some of the Fathers of the Church mention him, but his cult, especially in the

West, did not begin until the fourteenth and fifteenth centuries. Saint Teresa of Avila did much to extend devotion to Saint Joseph. *I do not know how anyone can think of the Queen of the Angels, during the time that she suffered so much with the Child Jesus, without giving thanks to Saint Joseph for the way he helped them. If anyone cannot find a master to teach him to pray, let him take this glorious Saint as his master, and he will not go astray.* Saint Teresa chose him as the chief Patron of her Order and said: *I do not remember ever having asked God through him for anything which I did not obtain. I never knew anyone who by invoking him did not advance exceedingly in virtue; for he assists in a wonderful way all who address themselves to him.*

His feast on the 19th of March was introduced in 1621 by Pope Gregory XV, and that of Saint Joseph the Worker, on the 1st of May, by Pope Pius XII in 1955. Even more recently his name was included in the Canon of the Mass by Pope John XXIII, and Pope John Paul II speaks of the protection Saint Joseph gives to the Church in his encyclical *Redemptoris Custos* in 1989, reminding us that he was declared Patron of the Universal Church by Pope Pius IX.

There is a certain parallel between the lives of Our Lady and Saint Joseph; both were chosen by God for a very special mission, participating as no other in the work of the Redemption and the mystery of the Incarnation. Both were eminently holy (though only Mary was conceived Immaculate); both were models of holy virginity. If Saint John the Baptist was sanctified in his mother's womb, perhaps it is not extravagant to think that Saint Joseph too would have been granted this privilege, and also that, like his Spouse, he is in Heaven with his glorified body. We do not know, but, as Duns Scotus, writing of the privileges of Mary, said,

Deus potuit; decuit, ergo fecit – God could do it; it was fitting, therefore He did it.

After so many centuries, this greatest of all the Saints is at last receiving the honour and love which is his due, to thank him for the care he took of Jesus and Mary during his life on earth and the care he now takes of all the children of God in the Church.

Blessed Kateri Tekakwitha

The Europeans who crossed the Atlantic to settle in the New World found many areas populated by different tribes of hardy, warlike people, to whom they gave the name of Red Indians. The Indian tribes – Sioux, Hurons, Iroquois, Mohawks, Algonquins, among others – were constantly in conflict with each other. Boys were brought up to be warriors; physical prowess and courage were the qualities they most admired. The French settlers who occupied the land around the great river which they called the Saint Lawrence included priests who went not only to take care of their own people but to preach the Christian faith to the Indians.

Early in the 17th century some of the Indians had already been converted, among them a young woman of the Algonquin tribe who was captured in a raid by the Iroquois and became the wife of the Chief. She passed on her Catholic faith to their two children, noticing that the little girl seemed to understand more than was usual at such an early age. The Chief, his wife and his infant son died in an epidemic of smallpox, leaving the little girl an orphan at the age of four. Her eyesight had been damaged by the disease and for this reason the relatives of her father – her uncle was now the Chief – called her *Tekakwitha*, meaning one who advances cautiously. She learned how to help with the women's duties and at times would slip away on her own to pray as her mother had taught her. The Iroquois raids on the neighbouring tribes continued until in 1666 an alliance was made between the Hurons and Algonquins and the French, who had organised an expeditionary force to subdue them.

Desire for baptism

Once the peace treaty had been concluded, three French priests visited the village, tending the sick and the wounded. In this first contact with Christians since her mother's death, Tekakwitha had no opportunity to speak to the priests, but she made up her mind then that she must be baptized. Some years elapsed during which the people of her tribe noticed her industriousness and readiness to give help wherever required. They could not however understand her persistent refusal to agree to the marriage arrangements they wished to make for her, and their consequent hostile attitude caused her considerable suffering. She continued patiently with her work, going into the forest each day to pray in solitude, asking for her own baptism and for the gift of faith for her people.

Joy and suffering

One of the missionary priests moved into the village where she lived, but his task was hampered by his knowing very little of the language; communication was limited to signs and drawings. However, by 1670 when he moved to another village, a considerable group of the Iroquois had begun to show interest in Christianity. Three years later the first of them were baptised. Tekakwitha could not join them. Her uncle, the Chief, and her other relatives were adamant in their refusal; many of the tribe were opposed to the new faith and persecution of the converts began. By 1674 the Christians left for La Prairie, further along the river, where a Christian village had been established. Again, Tekakwitha was left behind to face the opposition of her relatives. The priests from the mission still visited the village, bringing medical supplies, so Tekakwitha spoke to one of them asking to be baptised. The priest warned her of what she would have to undergo because of the anti-Christian atmosphere in the village, but seeing that she was prepared for this continued to give her instructions. When the priest, Fr Jacques de Lamberville, considered her to be ready for Baptism, he spoke with the elders of the village. The Chief was still totally opposed; without his consent Tekakwitha could do nothing. Then her prayers were answered in an unexpected way; another Chief, of greater authority than her uncle, came to visit the village. He himself had become a Catholic and spoke to the assembled villagers about his new faith. On hearing that Tekakwitha wished to be baptised he offered to be her godfather. Her uncle could not refuse, and at Easter on the 18th of April 1676 she received Baptism along with other members of the tribe. She was given the baptismal name of Kateri (Catherine). The hostility foretold by Fr de Lamberville began to show itself almost immediately, and ranged from verbal abuse to physical violence. Pressure was again put on her to marry, but she replied that she had Jesus as her only spouse. Kateri persevered, quietly fulfilling her tasks, treating everyone with her usual charity, praying for their conversion. She travelled with the tribe on the long hunting expeditions, working with the other women, preparing the skins, fetching water, putting up the tents. In order to pray with greater recollection she cut a cross into the trunk of a tree, kneeling before it on the ground.

La Prairie

Her return to the village brought renewed persecution. The priest in his concern spoke to some

Iroquois Catholics who happened to be passing through. They planned a means to help her escape to the Christian village of La Prairie, where certain other members of the tribe had already taken refuge. The journey was long, by canoe and on foot, with imminent danger of pursuit. Finally they reached the village, where Kateri was welcomed and taken in to live with one of the families. There she met an elderly woman who had known her mother. The Christians of La Prairie lived their faith with fervour, and the animosity between the tribes was eventually overcome by the bond of charity. Families prayed together, and a system was devised during the hunting season to remind them of Sundays and holydays so that they would not omit their religious duties. Some invented such severe penitential practices that the priests had to deter them; they had heard of the religious who lived a life of prayer and penance and wished to follow their example in their own way. Like the early Christians they shared their possessions and took care of those in need.

In a letter he had given to Kateri for Fr Cholenec, the priest of La Prairie, Fr de Lamberville had told him of Kateri's holiness. Her companions also informed him of her endurance of the persecution to which she had been subjected, and of the reputation for sanctity she had acquired among her people. Kateri cheerfully went on with the usual women's tasks and in addition undertook the religious education of the children, for whom she had a special sympathy and attraction. At the same time she was herself receiving classes in preparation for her own first Holy Communion. As before, she spent some time in prayer each day, erecting a cross made of branches near the river bank where she could be alone. She often visited the Blessed Sacrament in the chapel and showed great love for Our Lady. The villagers spoke of her outstanding charity to everyone, particularly the sick, of her unselfish generosity, her apostolic zeal and dedication to her work even though she was not strong in health. The date chosen for her first Holy Communion was Christmas Day. Fr Cholenec wrote of this occasion: *This young girl, uncivilized as she was, felt so filled with God and tasted such sweetness in this possession, that her whole exterior reflected this ... One did not have to be with her for long before being moved oneself and rekindled by this divine fire.*

As was customary, Kateri travelled with all the able-bodied members of the village to the winter hunting-grounds, accepting the hardships involved cheerfully, performing her duties energetically even though she was becoming weaker. Once back in the village she made more frequent visits to the Blessed Sacrament to make up for the long weeks away in the forest. At Easter she attended the Holy Week ceremonies for the first time, gaining a deeper insight into the sufferings of Christ in his Passion. A further offer of marriage came at this time, which Kateri again refused; the idea of dedicating oneself entirely to God's service was not yet understood by the Indians, even those who were Christian. When the opportunity arose, with a journey to the French city of Ville Marie (later Montreal), Kateri contacted the nuns of the Congregation of Notre Dame. After discussion with them and considering the matter in her prayer, Kateri knew that God wanted her to remain in her village, among her own people, living her normal life, sanctifying everything by making all she did an offering to God. She asked permission of the priest to make a vow of perpetual chastity. This she did on the feast of the Annunciation, the 25th of March 1679, the first of her people to do so. From that time her interior life of union with God grew deeper; she intensified her prayer and sought mortifications to offer as atonement. Many of the penances she performed were extraordinary, perhaps making up for the lack of a spirit of reparation in others.

The final offering

The following winter Kateri became seriously ill, remaining serene and joyful, accepting her condition as another way of fulfilling God's will. By Holy Week she was too infirm to be taken to the chapel and the priest brought Holy Communion to her; at this time she also renewed her baptismal vows. On the 17th of April, Wednesday of Holy Week, she died, attended by the priest and several women of the village. Her last words were, *Jesus, I love you.* She was twenty-four. Those present stated that at her death her face was transformed, becoming radiant and peaceful. Her burial place was marked with a wooden cross and, as the report of her sanctity spread from village to village, her grave became a place of pilgrimage both for her own Indian people and the white settlers.

Many cures and other miracles were soon attributed to her intercession, and she is said to have appeared in glory six days after her death to one of the missionaries, Fr Chauchetière, who afterwards wrote an account of her life and painted a portrait of her. More and more groups came on pilgrimage, and a Fr Charlevoix wrote at the time that *God no doubt wished, for our instruction and for the consolation of the lowly, to glorify his saints in proportion as they were tiny and obscure on earth.*

Her relics were transferred to Caughnawage, beside the Saint Lawrence. The inscription on the tomb, with her name and date of death – the 17th of April 1680 – describes her as *the most beautiful flower that has ever blossomed on the banks of the Saint Lawrence.*

The *Lily of the Mohawks*, as she came to be called, was beatified in Rome on the 22nd of June 1980 by Pope John Paul II. Speaking to the six hundred representatives of twenty Indian tribes attired in their traditional dress, the Holy Father said: *Holiness of life – union with Christ through prayer and works of charity – is not something reserved for a select few among the members of the Church. It is the vocation of everyone ... May you be inspired by the life of Blessed Kateri. Look to her for an example of fidelity; see in her a model of purity and love; turn to her in prayer for assistance.*

Her feast is celebrated in Canada on the 17th of April and in the United States on the 14th of July.

SAINT MARGARET MARY ALACOQUE

In the France of the seventeenth century the new, strict doctrine of Cornelius Jansen, Professor at Louvain University and Bishop of Ypres, began to take root. In order to counteract what he considered a scandalous laxity within the Church, Jansen preached a religion of severity and fear of God. His ideas were adopted by the French Abbot of Saint Cyran and became firmly established in the Cistercian convent of Port Royal, whose nuns were once described as being *as pure as angels and as proud as devils*.

The Jansenists held that original sin had totally corrupted human nature, hence everything natural was evil; the effects of grace were irresistible, therefore if God gives grace, man cannot sin; if He withholds it, man cannot do other than sin. Grace is given to a select few who will attain salvation; the vast majority are born to be damned. The Sacrament of Penance was ineffective unless accompanied by perfect contrition, and absolution was not to be given until after the penance had been fulfilled. Holy Communion was to be received when one was sufficiently worthy, as a reward for virtue; it was more meritorious not to approach this Sacrament than to receive it.

These harsh doctrines found many adherents, despite their being in opposition to the teachings of the Council of Trent upheld by Saint Charles Borromeo, Saint Philip Neri and the preachers of the Society of Jesus, who encouraged more frequent reception of the Sacraments as a means of bringing about a spiritual renewal among the faithful. Although Jansenism was condemned by the Church, the harmful effects lingered on, preventing souls from realising the immensity of God's love for mankind. The person chosen by Divine Providence to remind the world of this Love was the daughter of an ordinary family from a little village in Burgundy.

The early years – a preparation

Claude Alacoque, royal notary and judge, and his wife Philiberte lived in the village of Lautecour. They had seven children, of whom Margaret was the fifth. As was the custom, the child was baptised three days after birth. Her godmother, Madame de Fautrières, frequently invited Margaret to stay with her at the Château Corcheval where she would play in the surrounding woods and visit the little chapel to pray. From an early age she learned to have a great detestation of sin; it was enough for her to be told that something was displeasing to God for her to desist immediately.

Her carefree childhood days ended abruptly in Margaret's eighth year when her father died. As her mother was unable to attend to all the family affairs – she was trying to recover money owing to them by several of Claude's clients – Margaret was sent to live at a convent school, where she made her first Holy Communion. Although only nine she began to feel the need of solitude in order to pray, and often left her companions to find some quiet place. She became very ill when she was eleven and had to return to her family, where she remained an invalid for almost four years. Her mother told her to ask Our Lady to cure her, which Margaret did, promising then to join a religious order which had great devotion to Mary. Her recovery was instantaneous. For several years she continued to live with her mother and some relatives who, good enough people though they were, treated the mother and daughter very harshly, to the extent that Margaret would hide at times to avoid their less than kind ministrations. More kindly neighbours gave them food as they were allowed very little in the house. Margaret never mentioned their names, but referred to them as *true friends of my soul*, accepting her sufferings with serenity, and drawing strength from contemplating the Passion of Our Lord.

During this period of her life she was torn between her desire to follow the call of God and that of pleasing her mother, who urged her to marry as a way of escape for both of them. She began to perform severe penances in her endeavour to offer something to God, but continued to feel that she was being asked to give her entire life to his service. When her brother Chrysostome got married, Margaret knew that her mother would now be taken care of and that she could at last follow her vocation. Her decision became final when she was confirmed at the age of twenty-two. One day after Holy Communion she heard Our Lord within her telling her *I want you at Sainte-Marie*. This was the name by which the Visitation convents were known. These houses had been founded by Saint Francis de Sales and Saint Jeanne de Chantal. Her family pressed her to join the Ursuline order, as one of her cousins was a nun with the Ursulines, but Margaret knew that this was not for her. Eventually she persuaded Chrysostome to accompany her to the Visitation convent at Paray le Monial. Again she heard the voice in her soul: *It is here that I want you*. A month later she was permitted to enter.

In the following weeks, Margaret sought with docility to let herself be formed in the spirit of Saint Francis de Sales, seeking no special attention and wishing only to love Christ through suffering for him. She was told by her superior, Mother Thouvant, to place herself before Our Lord like a blank canvas ready for the painter. Unsure of what this meant, Margaret went to pray in the chapel before the Blessed Sacrament. There Our Lord made her understand that her soul was like the prepared surface on which He would paint the image of his suffering love. On one occasion when she was intending to perform a penance exceeding in severity the limits set by her superior, she was reproached in a vision by the Founder himself, Saint Francis de Sales, who told her that obedience was more pleasing to God than many austerities.

Two months after her arrival Margaret received the habit, on the 25th of August 1671. From then on she was known as Sister Margaret Mary, her confirmation name being added to the one given at Baptism. Our Lord made it known to her that she would be granted great graces and consolations; these so overwhelmed her that at times she was unaware of what was happening around her. The superiors were disconcerted; her enraptured prayer was not what was customary in the Order; they feared it could be a deceit of the devil. Their doubts were allayed by the gentle docility and humility of Sister Margaret Mary, who always obeyed immediately whenever any task was allotted to her, even during the time when she would normally have been praying in the chapel with the rest of the community. She remained united to God in all circumstances. She strove to live a spirit of mortification continually, always offering everything to Our Lord.

Victim of reparation
     Some things cost her a great deal – her abhorrence of cheese, for instance, which she continued to compel herself to eat, until forbidden by her

superiors as it was damaging her health. As time went on, God's graces increased in her soul, and when making her retreat before her profession Our Lord told her that He sought her as a victim, ready to sacrifice herself as a holocaust to his Heart in the fulfilment of his Will. Margaret Mary was very much afraid, knowing herself to be so unworthy of this great Love. Jesus then showed her his Wounds, telling her that Saint Francis of Assisi would be her special guide.

Our Lord accompanied her all the time, especially when during the retreat she was entrusted with looking after the convent's donkey and its foal, and with keeping them out of the vegetable garden. He gave her a wonderful insight into his Passion and Death and an insatiable desire to suffer in atonement. She wrote, *I cannot live one moment without suffering, but suffering in silence without consolation, alleviation or compassion.*

Doubts were raised in the convent when the time for her profession came. She was different from the rest because of her outstanding ecstasies, and tended to be distracted and clumsy in everyday life. *Lord,* she told him, *you will have me sent away!* His reply was, *Tell your superior that she need have no fear in receiving you, and if she will trust me, I will be your surety.* The sisters' decision to allow her to be professed was unanimous. Christ promised her that He would never leave her, and from that time she received the grace of an awareness of his continual presence in a way she had never experienced before. *I saw and felt him close to me and heard him better than I could have done with my bodily senses.*

The Sacred Heart

In carrying out her duties Margaret Mary had to undergo innumerable humiliations and sufferings, caused in part by her inability to overcome her own shortcomings, which she gladly accepted as yet another opportunity of offering reparation and love to God. Each morning she hastened to accompany him in the Blessed Sacrament, preparing herself with recollection when able to receive him in Holy Communion. Once, before receiving him, He made her see *his Sacred Heart shining like the sun, and as it were of an infinite immensity, and a tiny dark atom which was vainly attempting to approach the light until this living Heart drew it into itself.* The revelations made to Margaret Mary were numerous, preparing her as the victim of his Love.

In 1673 Our Lord explained a little of what He suffered in his Agony in Gethsemane: *It is here that I suffered more than in all the rest of my Passion, in seeing myself forsaken by heaven and earth, and charged with the sins of all mankind – no creature can comprehend the greatness of the torments I suffered at that time.* That same year on the 27th of December, the feast of Saint John, the beloved disciple who had been so close to the Love of Christ, Jesus made known the Love of his Heart for mankind: *My Divine Heart is so full of love for men, and especially for you, that unable any longer to keep within itself the flames of its burning Love it needs must spread them abroad through you.* He then took her heart, placed it into his own, and returned it to her. From then on she suffered an intense pain in her side which could never be alleviated.

A further vision showed her the Sacred Heart, bearing the Wound of the lance, encircled by a crown of thorns, with a cross above it. Our Lord gave her to understand that the instruments of the Passion were to show his infinite Love for us and his acceptance of all the outrages He would have to suffer in the Blessed Sacrament, as well as his great desire to be loved by us in return.

Margaret Mary was shown the Sacred Heart of Jesus on the first Friday of each month. On one of these occasions, Jesus told her that in return for his boundless love He received only ingratitude from men – an ingratitude which wounded him more than anything else in his Passion. He asked her at least to console him as far as she could. He then asked her to receive him in Holy Communion every first Friday, and to spend an hour from eleven o'clock till midnight on the eve, united in prayer with him in his Agony in the Garden, in order to make up in some way for the abandonment by his Apostles and the betrayal of Judas. After this vision Margaret Mary fell seriously ill; the Superior told her to ask Our Lord to cure her as a proof that the visions were authentic. She recovered rapidly and was given permission to fulfil the request of Our Lord.

Blessed Claude de la Colombière

Mother Saumaise, her Superior, felt at a loss as to how to guide this soul, so specially chosen by God; some priests whom she consulted thought the visions were pure imagination, or even worse, a satanic deception. Margaret Mary turned to Our Lord, who reassured her – He would send *his own servant* to whom she was to communicate everything He had revealed to her, and this person would be her spiritual guide.

In 1675 Blessed Claude de la Colombière came to Paray le Monial as superior of the Jesuits there. The first time he visited the convent Margaret Mary heard in her heart the locution, *This is he whom I send you.* He was appointed confessor to the nuns and, in obedience to her Superior, Margaret Mary told him everything, although reluctantly. When Blessed Claude was celebrating Holy Mass Christ made Margaret Mary see *his Sacred Heart like a burning furnace, and two other hearts which were going to be united with it, lost in that abyss.* He said, *It is thus that my pure Love unites these three hearts forever.* He told Margaret Mary that He wished her to tell Blessed Claude everything He had revealed to her.

On the octave of the feast of Corpus Christi, as it was by then called, Our Lord told her to ask Blessed Claude to do all he could to establish public devotion to his Sacred Heart. Margaret Mary heard these words: *Behold this Heart which has loved men so much that It has left nothing undone, exhausting and consuming itself in order to prove to them its love; and I receive from most men only ingratitude, as shown by their disrespect and sacrileges, and by the coldness and contempt which they show to me in this Sacrament of Love; and what I feel most keenly is that these are hearts which are consecrated to me.* Christ then asked for a special feast in honour of his Sacred Heart to be held on the Friday after the octave of Corpus Christi, a day on which the faithful should receive Holy Communion and make reparation for the insults He receives. Margaret Mary gave a detailed verbal and written account of this vision to Blessed Claude, who prayed and considered it carefully, and came to the conclusion that it was from God. The following Friday he dedicated himself to the Sacred Heart and began to spread the devotion among the people of Paray.

Margaret Mary was left without his support when Blessed Claude was sent to England in 1676 as chaplain to Mary of Modena, wife of King Charles II. The atmosphere was very anti-Catholic; Parliament had recently introduced the Test Act, by which all who held official positions had to swear an oath to uphold the teaching of the Church of England. The King's own brother, James, Duke of York, even had to resign his post as

Lord High Admiral as he refused to deny his faith by taking the oath. Blessed Claude lived in St James's Palace, the home of the Duke and Duchess of York. Officially the English were forbidden to attend the chapel in the palace where he preached, though many did. He preached there very frequently, giving clear explanations of Catholic doctrine and spreading devotion to the Sacred Heart.

He began to learn English and moved around the city visiting Catholics, and risking his life by doing so. He also visited King Charles, who was converted on his deathbed eight years later. Whilst in London, Blessed Claude felt the first symptoms of consumption and soon became very ill. His stay coincided with Titus Oates' 'Popish Plot' – the alleged plan of the Jesuits to assassinate the King, put the Catholic Duke of York on the throne, murder non-Catholics and bring in foreign troops to overrun the country. King Charles paid no heed to the rumours, but they had the effect of arousing even more bitter anti-Catholic feeling among the people. Blessed Claude was denounced as a Jesuit conspirator by someone who had pretended to be converted by him, and was arrested and thrown into prison. The reward for information about 'Jesuit conspirators' was one hundred pounds, a fortune in those days. Although his accusers could find no way of substantiating the charges, his life was in great danger as he had received converts into the Church, a capital offence under the Elizabethan penal laws which were still in force. When Louis XIV heard of the arrest he demanded his immediate release as Claude was a French citizen. He was then deported back to France. His brief sojourn in England had been enough to sow the seeds of devotion to the Sacred Heart; Mary of Modena was the first royal personage to request from the Pope the establishment of the devotion.

Several of the nuns were unwilling to believe in the visions, particularly when Our Lord asked Margaret Mary to make reparation for the sins against charity committed in that community; this drew down their anger and resentment, which showed itself in the subsequent treatment she received, causing her great suffering. She offered this in silence, humbly trying to make atonement to the suffering Christ.

In 1678, Mother de Saumaise, who had great sympathy with and appreciation of Margaret Mary, was moved to another convent where she began to propagate the devotion. Her successor at Paray, Mother Greyfié, soon drew her own conclusions regarding Sister Margaret Mary, since the other nuns were divided in their opinions. She tested Margaret, correcting and humiliating her, but quickly perceived the depth of her sanctity. Margaret Mary had a vision of the Seraphim surrounding the Sacred Heart of Jesus; they told her of their envy of her because she could suffer for love. This was the prelude to a time of great physical pain for which she gave thanks to God. Mother Greyfié asked her to request a complete cure for a specified time, again as a means of verifying the authenticity of the revelations. Her health was perfect for the stipulated time.

Development of devotion to the Sacred Heart

In 1681 Blessed Claude returned to Paray after two years at Lyons. Mother Greyfié noticed that when he died on the 15th of February 1682 Margaret Mary did not grieve, nor ask to do extra prayer and penance for the repose of his soul as she usually did for others. When asked the reason, she replied that he had no need, as he could now pray for them, being very high in

Heaven; instead she gave thanks to the Sacred Heart for the graces bestowed on Blessed Claude during his life and after his death. (He was beatified in 1929.)

After Mother Greyfié came Mother Melin, a gentle, holy person, appointed Superior in 1684. She selected Margaret Mary as her Assistant; shortly afterwards she was also made novice-mistress. She taught the young nuns how to love the will of God above all things, to be truly detached from everything in order to give themselves entirely to God, telling them that a soul without prayer is like a soldier without weapons. One of her great joys was to speak to them of the infinite Love of Jesus and foster devotion to his Sacred Heart. She make a sketch of the wounded Heart, surrounded by flames and encircled by the crown of thorns. On her feast day the novices made a small altar which they decorated, placing the sketch in the centre, and invited the rest of the community to pay homage to the Heart of Jesus. Most of the nuns refused, considering this an unjustifiable innovation, so Margaret Mary encouraged the young novices to continue to pray for the extension of the devotion.

The nuns' reservations were dispelled when the *Spiritual Retreat* of Blessed Claude was read aloud in the refectory; his words in praise of the *holy soul* who had been favoured with the visions of *this Heart which has so loved men* had a wonderful effect. The next Friday after the octave of Corpus Christi one of the older nuns made a small altar, placing on it a copy of the symbolic drawing of the Sacred Heart, and all the nuns this time attended the devotions. They then decided to build a chapel specifically for this devotion in the grounds of the convent, raising the money by selling garden produce; several noted that the garden had never previously been so fruitful.

Devotion to the Sacred Heart now became more widespread in France and elsewhere. Margaret Mary knew that she had accomplished the task required of her, and when she became ill in 1690 after her retreat, she asked one of the nuns to destroy the notebooks in which she had written her account of the revelations. Fortunately the nun did not do so, asking her instead to put them at the disposal of the Superior. The doctor who had attended her on previous occasions did not attach undue importance to her illness, and although she asked for the Holy Viaticum the nuns did not consider this necessary. She deteriorated rapidly over the next few hours and at last they sent for the priest, who came and administered the Last Sacraments. The superior wanted to summon the doctor again, but Margaret Mary told her, *I want nothing now, Mother, only God alone, and to lose myself in the Sacred Heart of Jesus.* Whispering the name of Jesus, she died on the seventeenth of October, 1690.

The process of beatification and canonization was delayed because of the troubles in France. She was beatified in 1864 by Pope Pius IX, and canonized in 1920 by Benedict XV. One of the great men in France who had petitioned for her beatification was Prince Talleyrand, then Bishop of Autun, who later apostatized, causing great harm to the Church. Almost fifty years later he died, having retracted his errors, and was reconciled to the Church, receiving the Sacraments with faith and humility. Pope Gregory XVI commented that this was a proof that acts of pious faith never pass unnoticed in Paradise.

One of the last pieces of advice given by Saint Margaret Mary was this: *to become holy we just have to love him … what is there to hinder us, since we have hearts with which to love?*

SAINT MARGARET OF SCOTLAND

Saint Margaret, who became Queen of Scotland, was born in Hungary in 1046, where her father, Edward, heir to the English throne, had been sent for safety as a child. Edward had the good fortune to be brought up in the court of St Stephen, King of this recently converted and very devout country, and eventually married Princess Agatha, the Queen's sister. Margaret was the youngest of the three children they had – Edgar, Christina and Margaret – and their life as children in Hungary seems to have been very happy. The influence of the saintly King lived on for many years after him, and must have played a great part in Margaret's later life.

When Margaret was eight years old, her father was invited to return to England, since the reigning monarch, Edward the Confessor, had no heir, and his nephew and namesake Edward was the next in line.

Life in England

The family left the court of one saintly ruler for that of another. They were very well received by the King, and Margaret's happy childhood continued undisturbed until her father died an untimely death in 1057. Saint Edward took care of the widowed mother and her children, keeping them at the court, where Margaret again learned a good deal which was to stand her in good stead in the years to come.

Some time earlier Saint Edward had received another royal prince into his court – the exiled Malcolm, heir to the Scottish throne, whose father

Duncan had been murdered by the notorious Macbeth, one of King Duncan's generals. Macbeth held on to power for seventeen years, until with the aid of troops provided by Saint Edward, Malcolm was able to win back his kingdom and was proclaimed King of Scotland at Scone in 1057.

Saint Edward's personal sanctity, wisdom and charity in governing his country made a deep impression on Margaret. One of his great works, of course, was the building of the great monastic church of St Peter in London, which took many years to build, being completed and consecrated at Christmas in 1065. The splendid ceremony was attended by people of all ranks, but its founder lay dying, and a few days later, his body was laid to rest in this beautiful Westminster Abbey he had built.

Escape from danger

After Saint Edward's death many of the people of England wanted Margaret's brother Edgar as King, but as he was young and had been born in a foreign country he had neither the power nor the resources to withstand his rival, Count Harold. As is well known from this famous chapter in English history, the new King reigned for scarcely a year, since William of Normandy, who also had a claim to the English throne, defeated Harold at Hastings in 1066. Edgar realised that the lives of his family were now in jeopardy, and decided to take his mother and sisters back to Hungary. Shortly after they had set sail they were caught in a violent storm which drove the ship quite dramatically off course; they landed eventually with some difficulty on the east coast of Scotland.

Malcolm the King was celebrating with his chieftains after a successful raid over the Border into

England when news was brought that *a ship full of noble lords and ladies had been driven onto the shore of Fife*. The King immediately left his fortress at Dunfermline to meet the unfortunate travellers, whom *he conducted to his palace with so much sweetness and goodness that they had reason from that happy moment to bury in oblivion all their former misfortunes*.

When William *the Conqueror* heard of the whereabouts of Edgar and his sisters he sent a message to Malcolm demanding their return. Malcolm refused. William was infuriated and ordered his generals to attack. Malcolm defeated first Roger, the Norman general in Northumberland, then Richard, Earl of Gloucester, and also William's brother Odo, the Earl of Kent. Only then did William agree to terms of peace.

Queen of Scotland

From the first moment he met her, Malcolm had been very much attracted by Margaret. She was beautiful, accomplished and virtuous. Accordingly he sought her brother's permission to marry her and *he dealt with her brother, Edgar, until he said yea*. Margaret gave her own consent and the wedding was celebrated with great rejoicing at Dunfermline in 1070, when the young princess was crowned Queen of Scotland. The contrast between the court of Malcolm the warrior-king and those of England and Hungary must have been quite extraordinary. Margaret rose to the challenge with great fortitude, determined with God's help to win over the war-like people who were now her own. Through her love and gentleness she gradually softened the ruggedness of Malcolm's character; he had been known as the Great Chief *merciless to his enemies, ruling his followers with a rod of iron.*

Margaret next turned her attention to her new

home, introducing bit by bit some of the dignity of Saint Edward's court. She had brought many treasures with her from England, (among them being the Holy Rood, a richly- wrought black cruciform reliquary containing a relic of the True Cross, for the reception and custody of which her son David founded Holyrood Abbey). The great chambers of Dunfermline and Edinburgh castles she had decorated with beautiful wall hangings; gold and silver vessels were used at the royal table, and Margaret is also said to have obtained panes of glass for the windows as protection from the weather. These were considered a great treasure at the time, and were taken from place to place whenever the royal family travelled.

Little by little the example of his wife's love, piety and virtue led Malcolm to a more Christian way of life. Margaret was not afraid of speaking clearly when the need arose, *freely telling him that if the Supreme Sovereign should find crimes in monarchs, their crowns would not be a buckler strong enough to withstand His thunders.*

Her apostolic concern for others did not allow Margaret to be content with helping only her husband in his personal life. She *let him know that in his kingdom vice was in esteem and virtue in contempt, particularly setting before his eyes the abuses that were crept in and conjuring him to give a speedy remedy to them; to reform justice; to cut short the delays and wranglings that rendered suits at law endless; to punish the manifest corruptions of the courts of justice; to order a despatch of the affairs of the poor before all others; to repress the insolence of the soldiery who ruined the people and laid waste the country; to make his subjects enjoy plenty, peace and liberty; to appease quarrels; to banish incontinency; to make a choice of priests eminent in learning and virtue to preach the Mysteries of our Faith and administer the Holy Sacraments, assuring him that much noble and holy government would be a lodestone to draw him both the favours of heaven and the blessing of his subjects.* It is interesting to note that Margaret did not confine herself to pointing out the problems, but suggested several very practical solutions.

Malcolm's greatness of character is shown by his humility in listening to and following the advice of his wife. His pride in her learning and wisdom is very touching. *Although he could not read he would turn the pages of the books she used for study or prayer and whenever he realised that she was very fond of one of them, this one too he used to look at with special affection, kissing it and often taking it into his hands. Sometimes he sent for a worker in precious metals whom he commanded to ornate that volume with gold and gems, and when the work was finished, the King used to carry it to the Queen as a kind of proof of his devotion.* One of these volumes is a beautifully illuminated copy of the Gospels, now kept in the Bodleian Library at Oxford.

Margaret provided a practical lesson on the virtue of mercy by herself paying the ransom for captives brought back by Malcolm after his victorious campaigns. When her own funds were insufficient she would even borrow what she could from her attendants, and also helped herself quite happily from her husband's personal treasury. Fortunately, Malcolm always took this *borrowing* in good part! The King and Queen both attended personally to the wants of many needy folk early each day, supplying them with food and other necessities. Malcolm learned that mercy and concern for the less fortunate is not a sign of weakness, but rather the mark of a great character, and the only way to rule as a Christian King.

The Royal Family

The royal couple had eight children – Edward, Edmund, Ethelred, Edgar, Alexander, David, Matilda (or Maud), and Mary. Margaret was a devoted mother and took great care with their upbringing. However, she did not spoil them, and instructed their tutor *to curb the children, to scold them and to whip them whenever they were naughty as frolicsome childhood will often be.* The advice does not seem to have done them any harm... Margaret made sure that the lives of her children's teachers were such that their example as well as their words would be a positive influence. The Douai Chronicle gives a list of the instructions she left for her children:

1. To die a thousand deaths rather than commit one mortal sin.

2. To give sovereign honour and absolute adoration to the Most Holy Trinity, and to have particular respect and veneration for the Most Blessed Virgin, the Mother of God.

3. To be charitable to the poor, to protect orphans and relieve them in their necessities.

4. To abhor all obscene language and uncleanness.

5. To converse with persons of blameless lives and to follow their judgements and counsels.

6. To be firm, constant and unchangeable in the maintenance of the Catholic Faith.

Parents today, of course, could hardly give better advice to their children.

The example of these parents was quite clearly reflected in the lives of their children. Matilda (Maud) became the wife of Henry I of England, and was called by her subjects *Maud, the good Queen.* Ethelred became Abbot of Dunkeld, and the three younger sons succeeded each other as Kings of Scotland. Edgar (the

Peaceable) was described as *a sweet and amiable man, like his kinsman the holy King Edward in every way.*

He was followed by Alexander *the Fierce*, who seems to have inherited a fair share of his father's temperament. He was *a lettered and godly man, very humble and amiable towards the clerics and regulars, but terrible beyond measure to the rest of his subjects; a man of large heart, exerting himself in all things to the utmost of his strength.* David, the youngest, reigned for twenty-nine years and is remembered as the best of Scotland's kings, who *in his days illumined his lands with kirks and abbeys.* One of the sons did go astray for some time, but like the prodigal in the Parable repented and lived an exemplary life from then on.

Reforms

Besides taking care of her family, Margaret's concern was extended to those around her − first of all to the members of the royal court, and then to the whole kingdom. Accustomed as Malcolm's followers were to living in battle conditions, their manners left something to be desired. Without offending them Margaret managed to refine their behaviour − for example on an early occasion requesting them gently to remain seated at table until grace had been said, and then inviting them to a cup of her own wine. From then on the meals were more dignified, and the Queen's grace cup was passed round at each feast. Margaret ensured that the King was always served by suitable attendants who were to escort him in state whenever he went out of the castle. The royal household became much more like those to which she had been accustomed and this, undoubtedly through her powers of persuasion and determination. Margaret *knew so well how to join gentleness with firmness, and all those who had the honour*

*to serve her had a particular respect to her person, so that
none durst do anything unhandsome in her presence, nor
utter even in her absence a word that had the least relish
of impurity.*

The Queen passed on the talents and accomplishments she had received – she was an expert at fine embroidery and set about teaching the daughters of the nobility. Another part of her self-appointed task was social reform and an improvement in the standard of living of her people. With her characteristic gift for organisation she favoured establishing trading links with other countries whose goods and manufactures would be welcome in Scotland. *It was due to her that the merchants who came by land and sea from various countries brought along with them for sale different kinds of precious wares which until then were unknown in Scotland. And it was at her instigation that the natives of Scotland purchased from these traders clothing of various colours with ornaments to wear, so that, from this period, through her suggestion, new costumes of different fashion were adopted, the elegance of which made the wearers appear like a race of new beings.*

Margaret's concern for the less fortunate did not remain a pious sentiment. Being a generous woman, like all mothers of large families who always have room for more, she personally took care of nine orphans – *the Queen's bairnies*, as they were called. Then there were the pilgrims who travelled to St Andrews to pray at the shrine of their patron Saint. She had hostels built for them on either side of the Forth, and provided *the Queen's ferry* to enable them to cross – the ferrymen not being permitted to ask for remuneration from the pilgrims. In Rome too there was a hostel for Scottish pilgrims, founded by the King and Queen.

The welfare of the Church

Having been brought up in Hungary where the Catholic faith was very much alive, and then in England – at that time well called *Our Lady's Dowry*, the country being still very devout and loyal to the Holy See – Margaret was accustomed to living in the atmosphere of a deep and lively faith. Scotland too had a great Catholic tradition, dating back to Saint Ninian in the fifth century and later to Saint Columba and his monks, who founded the monastery at Iona and spread the Faith throughout the land. But then had come the invaders from the lands to the North, pagans and fierce fighters who attacked on all sides, murdering, destroying and plundering. The monasteries with their sacred vessels and artistic treasures were a prime target. Eventually Northumbria fell into the power of the Norsemen, so that Scotland became cut off from the rest of Christendom. When Margaret came, she found that while the people held to the essentials of their Faith – the Mass, the Sacraments – abuses and strange practices had crept in. The monasteries, which had been the main centres of learning, lay pillaged and vacant, and the country lived in a certain isolation from the rest of the Catholic world.

Margaret began her plan of restoration by having a beautiful church built at Dunfermline, dedicated to the Blessed Trinity. She also rebuilt the monastery at Iona and supplied it with sacred vessels, with her own hands making vestments in her palace. *Copes for the cantors, chasubles, stoles, altar cloths and other priestly vestments and church ornaments were always to be seen, either already made of an admirable beauty, or in the course of preparation.* For God, nothing was too much or too good.

The material aspects of improvement however,

were the least of her problems. Scotland still had to be restored to full communion with Rome. Nothing daunted her, and she wrote for advice and help to Lanfranc, the Archbishop of Canterbury. Lanfranc was overjoyed. In reply he wrote: *The brief space of a letter cannot unfold the great gladness with which thou hast filled my heart, when I have read the letter which thou hast sent to me, Queen beloved of God.* He sent three learned monks to assist the Queen, promising his prayers and asking for hers.

A council was summoned, to be attended by the leading churchmen of Scotland, by Lanfranc's monks and the King and Queen. Malcolm did not take part in the discussions – he was no student of theology – but he provided an indispensable service as interpreter. He was fluent both in Latin and English, thanks to his long exile, as well as his native Gaelic.

Margaret raised the points at issue, starting with the Lenten fast, which the Scots then began on the first Monday of Lent, instead of on Ash Wednesday, thus having a thirty-six-day Lent instead of the customary forty. The practice of receiving Holy Communion at Easter had also become neglected. When Margaret asked those attending the Council the reason for this, they replied: *Since we admit that we are sinners, we fear to approach that Mystery lest we should eat and drink judgement to ourselves*. Margaret, who was familiar with the Gospels and knew her theology, answered with her usual clear logic. *Shall no-one who is a sinner taste that Holy Mystery? If so, then it follows that no-one at all should receive It, for no-one is free from sin, and if no-one ought to receive It, why did Our Lord make this pronouncement in the Gospel 'except you eat the Flesh of the Son of Man and drink His Blood, you shall not have life in you'? It is the man who, without Confession or penance, but carrying with him defilement of his sins, presumes to approach the sacred Mysteries, such a one, I say it is, who eats and drinks judgement to himself.* And so with all the other differences – some unauthorised rites at Mass, non-observance of the Sunday rest, unlawful marriages – each one was dealt with in the same clear, logical way. Those who had supported the errors changed their views, *willingly consenting to adopt all she had recommended.* Through Margaret's untiring efforts Catholic practice was revived in Scotland, particularly the custom of frequent reception of the Sacraments of Penance and the Holy Eucharist.

Life of piety

One could wonder how Margaret, a busy wife, mother and Queen, found the time and energy to carry out not only the duties proper to her state, but to do very much more. The answer lies in her relationship with God. Hers was a life of prayer – daily attendance at Holy Mass, setting aside some time for prayer, frequently receiving the Sacrament of Penance and the Body of Our Lord in Holy Communion, and living with an awareness of God's presence all the time, so that whatever she was engaged in would be done in his company. She must have been a woman of great fortitude – also one with a good sense of humour – to cope with life in two countries which were both foreign to her, and adapting herself to the ways of the somewhat unruly subjects she acquired by her marriage to their King.

Her piety was based on a sound knowledge of the doctrine of the Church, acquired through reading and study. This is what enabled her to assist others who were misguided; her gentleness combined with firmness, when necessary, always achieved its purpose without hurting those she was trying to change.

Living amidst great wealth, Margaret was very generous to others yet allowed herself no self-indulgence or lavish caprice. Her own meals were very frugal but she entertained her guests well. Throughout her life she always tried to respond to God's grace in whatever circumstances she found herself, trusting in his help in order to fulfil her duties, from the greatest affairs of state to the little homely details of every day.

Her death

Towards the end of her life – she was only forty-six when she died in 1093 – she became very ill, suffering great pain and gradually growing weaker. At this time William Rufus of England made a surprise attack on Alnwick Castle, putting all the occupants to the sword. Malcolm demanded restitution. William refused. Malcolm then beseiged the castle and eventually the English surrendered, offering to hand over the keys to the Scottish King. The soldier who presented the keys on the end of a spear treacherously stabbed Malcolm to death. Edward, his eldest son, immediately continued the battle and was also killed. The Scottish forces withdrew, sorrowfully carrying away the bodies of their King and his heir for burial.

Edgar hurried back from the battlefield to his mother's bedside. By this time Margaret had already received the Last Sacraments and asked for the Black Cross – the Holy Rood – to be brought to her. When Edgar entered, she asked, *How are the King and my Edward?* To avoid increasing her sufferings, her son replied, *They are well.* Margaret, who had tried to persuade her husband not to go to war on that occasion, fearing some disaster, realised the truth. *I know how it is*, she said, and then offered up this sorrow: *I thank*

Thee, Almighty God, that in sending me so great an affliction in the last hour of my life, Thou wouldst purify me from my sins, as I hope, by Thy mercy.

Her last words were those used in preparation for receiving Our Lord in Holy Communion – *Lord Jesus Christ, Son of the Living God, by the will of the Father and the work of the Holy Spirit, Your Death brought life to the world, deliver me …* and then she died, four days after her husband and her eldest son.

The prayer ends with the words *keep me faithful to Your teaching, and never let me be parted from You.* St Margaret's final prayer was answered.

Her body and that of Malcolm were buried in their church of The Holy Trinity at Dunfermline. Her tomb became a place of pilgrimage, many miracles being worked through her intercession. Pope Innocent IV canonized her in 1251 after a petition from King Alexander III of Scotland in the name of his subjects.

During the Reformation the relics of St Margaret and her husband were rescued before the Shrine was destroyed, and taken to Spain. King Philip II had them placed in a chapel in the Escorial palace near Madrid.

Margaret, the wife, mother and Queen who became a saint, has strong links with Hungary, with England and Scotland, and in this way is surely an excellent protectress to intercede for us in these present times when Pope John Paul II has been consistently asking for prayers and initiatives to be directed in a particular way towards the re-evangelisation of Europe.

SAINT MARIA GORETTI

When Saint María Goretti is mentioned, the first thought that springs to mind is usually that she is a saint because she was a martyr. In fact the converse is much nearer the truth – she is a Martyr because she was a Saint. For anyone who has attained the use of reason there is no such thing as *instant sanctity*, just as no-one wins an Olympic gold medal the first time they set foot in a sports stadium. Regular intense practice is required to make a *champion* either on the merely human plane or on the supernatural level. María (Marietta to her family and friends) achieved this level of sanctity before she was even twelve years old.

The little girl was born on the 16th of October 1890 in Corinaldo, Italy, and the following day was baptized María Teresa. She was the third of seven children, one of whom, Antonio, the eldest, died soon after he was born. Her parents Luigi and Assunta were poor; Assunta tells that very often they were really hungry. There was little work for Luigi in Corinaldo, so the family moved in 1897 and eventually settled in Conca delle Ferriere near Nettuno, with the hope of returning to Corinaldo when things improved.

Family difficulties

Matters took a turn for the worse when Luigi became ill and died in 1900, leaving Assunta with six young children to rear. Marietta was very close to her father, and what remained very clear in her mother's memory was how the girl would always stop by the cemetery on her way home and kneel to pray for him.

Even after praying the rosary at night with the rest of the family she would always say another, specially for her father, *in case he was in Purgatory*. Luigi's death had occurred before María made her first Holy Communion when she was almost eleven, and so, since he could not be with her, she offered it for him. She had made her first Confession and been confirmed at the age of six.

After Luigi's death the landowner had suggested that Assunta could look after the Serenellis, a widower and his son, who would do much of the work in the fields. Marietta was then in charge of most of the housework as Assunta too worked in the fields. The girl showed a maturity unusual in one so young. The work was tiring, but she never complained, and was a great support for her mother, encouraging her by saying that soon they would all be grown up and would be able to help her. Her mother admits that sometimes because of being tired and worried she would lose her temper with Marietta, who never made excuses for herself and even took the blame for things her brothers and sisters had done. Whenever Marietta received a present from friends – usually something to eat – she always gave it to her mother and the other children. Very often she would forgo her own share, saying that she did not feel like it at the moment – a considerable sacrifice for a child when food was so scarce.

A mother's influence

There was no possibility of Marietta's attending school, partly because of distance but mainly because the family needed her at home; as a result, she therefore never learned to read or write. All she knew was from her parents, especially her mother, who like her daughter had herself never been to school. Assunta felt very clearly that the role of parents is primarily to do all they can to help their children get to Heaven. She taught them how to pray, how to love God above all things and to accept his Will with serenity. She brought up all the children with sound ideas on faith and morals – if something was an offence against God, then one rejected it firmly. When asked why she insisted upon the children's going to Sunday Mass when the church was seven miles away and the walk took some two hours each way, she just said, *And why not?*

With her example, the young Gorettis grew in faith, fortitude and many other virtues. People noticed how recollected Marietta was during Mass, and saw how she helped to explain doctrine to her young brothers and sisters, remembering what she had learned from her mother and from sermons by the parish priest. Assunta recalled how Marietta was always obedient – the one particular thing she saw as special in her eldest daughter. One of her brothers said afterwards that even if they tried to get her to disobey she never would.

The children were taught to love and value purity, to avoid conversations or anything that could harm this virtue and be an offence against God.

Before her first Communion Marietta made a retreat given in the parish for the occasion and was deeply impressed by what the priest had said about the Passion of Our Lord. She went home and told her mother he had said that when we commit sin we renew that Passion; she had made the resolution to avoid sin at any cost. The family also noticed that after her first Confession she was trying to be better, and in order to prepare for Holy Communion she would pray more and do her work around the house even more carefully. Marietta received Holy Communion only three or four times before her death, but as her soul was so well disposed she was very receptive to the infinity of grace given by the Sacrament.

To die, rather than to sin

To all who knew her Marietta was a normal, happy child, pleasant and refined in her dealings with everyone, always modest in her speech, attire and attitude. She was reserved towards the Serenellis, especially Alessandro, the nineteen-year-old son, who she said later had tried to tempt her into sin. The Serenellis had a very different outlook on life from the Gorettis. The father was irritated by the strict honesty of the others. Assunta was upset by the type of pictures Alessandro had put up in his room – pictures with which he claimed he *didn't see anything wrong*. She pitied him because, as she said, *the poor boy had no mother to look after him*. Alessandro made a second attempt with Marietta, who again refused and did all she could to avoid him.

She mentioned nothing of this to her mother, knowing there was nothing she could do for her; they could not leave the house – there was nowhere else for them to go, nor would the Serenellis leave. Also, Alessandro had threatened to kill her if she told anyone what he had said. From taking pleasure in reading indecent publications he had fallen to the level of wanting to force an innocent child into grave sin. Her refusals made him more determined.

On the 5th of July Marietta had told her mother how much she was looking forward to receiving Holy Communion the next day – having already begun her preparation. That day the Serenellis and Assunta were busy threshing beans while Marietta stayed indoors to work and take care of her baby sister. On his way out,

Alessandro had announced that his shirt needed mending and asked if Marietta could do it; he had left the shirt and some material to repair it in his room. Marietta fetched it and sat on the terrace outside to sew, with her baby sister asleep nearby.

By some instinct she knew that her time of trial had come. She had pleaded with her mother to stay at home that day instead of going to the fields. Assunta was surprised, being unaware of the situation, and as Marietta did not appear to be ill and there was a great deal of work to be done, she went out to the fields with the Serenellis. Marietta prayed to Our Lady to help her.

Early in the afternoon Alessandro made an excuse to go back to the house and asked Assunta to take over the oxen for him. He went to his room, passing Marietta without speaking to her. Then he came out and called her. Marietta did not move. Angrily he called her again, then came and caught her by the arm, stuffing a rag into her mouth to prevent her from screaming. Once inside he slammed the door. Marietta struggled and managed to speak – *Not sin, it is against God's will; take care Alessandro, or you will go to hell.*

Alessandro had planned his moment well. The noise of the threshing would prevent the girl's cries from being heard, and he had ensured she would have to be in the house by asking her in front of everyone to mend his shirt. Everyone else was occupied in the field. He had not counted on the fortitude of the young girl. In his anger at being thwarted, Alessandro snatched a ten-inch knife and struck her over and over again – fourteen times. Marietta fell to the floor. Alessandro left her and, barely conscious, she managed to drag herself to the door and call for help.

The first thing Assunta heard was the baby crying,

so she realized Marietta had left it alone on the terrace. Alessandro's father heard Marietta cry out and called to another man working with them. When they found her covered in blood they thought she had had an accident. They placed her gently on a bed, unconscious. They managed to bring her round and Marietta asked for her mother, who asked her what had happened. *Alessandro did it*, she told her. When Assunta, horrified, asked why, she replied, *He wanted me to commit sin and I would not*. Again, when her friend Teresa Cimarelli asked her what had happened, she said, *He wanted me to commit a bad sin; I kept saying no, no!*

Forgiveness

The youth had gone to his room, and was pretending to be asleep. The ambulance arrived, as well as the police, who arrested Alessandro. The drive to the hospital along the uneven roads caused Marietta great pain. It was eight o'clock when they reached the hospital. She was parched with thirst, having lost so much blood, but nothing could be given to her as they were preparing to operate. She offered this suffering up in addition to the rest of her pain. A priest came to hear her Confession before the operation.

When she awoke she tried to console and encourage her mother, who then had to leave her for the night on doctor's orders. Marietta was deprived even of the consolation of her mother's presence during her last hours. Assunta stayed all night awake, sitting in the ambulance, hoping and praying.

On the morning of the 6th of July she was allowed in early and found her daughter looking lovingly at the picture of Our Lady on the wall. The nuns of the hospital had decorated the room with flowers in preparation for the moment when the priest would bring the Holy Viaticum and anoint her. Before giving her Holy Communion he spoke to her of Jesus forgiving those who crucified him and asked if she was able to forgive Alessandro. Immediately she replied, *Oh yes, I forgive him for the love of Jesus, and want him to be in Heaven with me*. She then received Holy Communion.

She had spoken of how she was looking forward to thus receiving Our Lord, but little thought it would be the last time before she saw him face to face in Heaven. When others asked her about Alessandro she said very quickly, *May God forgive him as I have forgiven him*.

Despite the efforts of the doctor Marietta's life was ebbing away. Assunta was by her bedside, giving her a crucifix which she kissed and telling her to prepare to meet her Creator. Before losing consciousness she called out for her father and then, in delirium, re-lived the moments of the attack, crying out, *What are you doing, Alessandro? Don't touch me or you'll go to hell*. Shortly after three o'clock she struggled as if resisting her attacker and fell back dead.

When Assunta was called to give evidence during Alessandro's trial, those present were amazed and moved to hear her beseeching the judge to have pity on the young man whom she too had forgiven wholeheartedly. Her logic was – *Why can't people pardon him when Marietta was the first to forgive him and Our Lord has already pardoned him? He committed a grave sin but God has brought great good out of it*. Marietta was a worthy daughter of such a mother. The young man testified to Marietta's purity and holiness when asked what he thought of her. *She was wholly innocent*, he said, *she knew no evil, she is a Saint*.

Twenty-five years after Alessandro had served his

prison sentence he made his way to the presbytery in Corinaldo. To his amazement Assunta opened the door – she was now the housekeeper for the priests there. Quietly he asked her, *Do you forgive me, Assunta?* She replied simply, *If God has forgiven you, do you think I will not?* She asked the parish priest if Alessandro could stay for the evening. It was Christmas Eve. They went to Holy Communion together at Midnight Mass.

Both Assunta and Alessandro were present at Marietta's canonization in the Holy Year 1950. In his address, Pope Pius XII encouraged parents and young people to have recourse to the young Saint to strengthen them in their fidelity to Christ in living the virtue of holy purity.

SAINT MARTIN DE PORRES

The first recorded information about Saint Martin is from the baptismal register of Lima Cathedral, Peru, 9th December 1579. He is registered there as *the son of Ana Velasquez, freed woman, name of father unknown.* The baptism took place in the church of Saint Sebastian, the ceremony performed by Fr Antonio Polanco the parish priest.

Right from the start Martin and his sister Juana suffered from the double disadvantage of being mulatto, generally despised at the time by those not of mixed race, and from the misfortune of being illegitimate – without the care of a true family. Ana worked hard to support the children, often scolding Martin, who never seemed able to resist the temptation to give away whatever he had to those whom he thought were even poorer than themselves.

The children's father, Juan de Porres, a Spanish nobleman, eventually acknowledged them and took them with him to Guayaquil, Ecuador, where he had settled some five years previously. Martin was then provided with a tutor and learned to read and write. Two years later Juan was appointed Governor of Panama. He returned to Lima to receive his letters of appointment from the Viceroy, leaving Juana in the care of his uncle in Guayaquil. Martin now stayed with his mother in Lima and Juan departed for Panama. Ana brought him up in the Catholic faith, and he was confirmed by the Archbishop of Lima, (Saint) Turibius of Mongrovejo.

When he was about ten, he started work as an

apprentice to Mateo Pastor, who sold spices and medicinal herbs while being also in the service of the local barber-surgeon, Marcelo Rivero. Through this apprenticeship Martin developed skills in healing, and attended to everyone who asked for his help, rich or poor, Spanish, Indian, Mestizo or Mulatto; to him, each was a person who deserved his care. At night he used to study in his room, and pray. For this he used to ask his landlady for candle-ends. Wondering how he used up so many, one night she looked through a crack in the door to find him kneeling in prayer before the crucifix. By the time he was fifteen he knew that God wanted him to live a life of complete dedication to him, and he approached the superior of the Dominican Priory of the Rosary, asking to be admitted as a 'donatus', a tertiary – he did not feel worthy to be a priest or lay-brother – just to work in the service of the monks in whatever tasks might be asked of him. Martin was accepted and given the white tunic with leather belt, but was told he would have to wait many years before being a full member of the Order.

In the Priory

The Priory was large, housing three hundred priests and students. His first responsibility was that of barber, a tiring job which entailed his being on his feet all day. Martin used his work and other occupations as a way of living in God's presence, offering it to him joyfully. Soon he had need of his medical experience when given the post of infirmarian. This made even greater demands on him, as he had to attend to the workers on the Priory farm in Limatambo, a few miles from the city, as well as the occupants of the monastery. In addition, patients came to him from Lima itself.

During an epidemic of fever he spent his days and nights carefully attending to the sick, many of whom felt that their recovery was not due solely to the medical ability of their infirmarian, but to divine help working through him. The doctor had warned one of the sick priests that his death was imminent. When Martin came to see him, he told him, *Don't worry, Father, you are not going to die for a long time yet.* The doctor was astonished to find the patient fully recovered a few days later and going about his normal duties. The only comment he could make was − it is a miracle. Those whom Martin tended felt that his devoted service made him seem to multiply himself; no-one was left unattended however many there were.

The charity of Brother Martin

For nine years Martin continued serving God through his fellow-men with no special bond uniting him to the Order. He was filled with joy when the Prior informed him that he could be professed in 1603. As time passed, his reputation for charity in looking after those in need increased, and with it, the number of those who sought his aid. He even had patients in the cloister and in his own cell. He slept on the floor. When no more patients could be accommodated there, as he was unwilling to turn anyone away he asked Juana his married sister for her help. Like her brother, she made room for them in her home. Martin then had to go on foot every day to take care of them. Whilst healing the bodies of his patients, Martin worked tirelessly to bring their souls closer to God; his service was because of his love for Christ, who died for all mankind; his aim, to act as co-redeemer with him. He made the words of Christ *Whatever you do to the least of my brethren, you do to me* a motive power in his life, always finding ways to help when others perhaps considered it impossible.

The plight of the numerous homeless children in Lima had defeated the efforts of the authorities; through God's help, Martin had two orphanages built, and found the necessary staff, teachers and funds. He begged for and obtained large sums which he distributed to the many poverty-stricken people living in the slum areas; he assisted priests whose parishes were too poor to support them; he provided food for a garrison of soldiers, taking it to them several times a week on a journey of over four miles.

His reputation for holiness spread through Lima, because of the way he taught love by his example. Testifying to his sanctity, one of the monks, Cipriano de Medina, said of him, *his cell was the office of charity,* and Brother Juan de la Torre said that although his name was Brother Martin de Porres, what fitted better would have been Martin de la Caridad.

A field of apostolate very dear to him was that among the convicted criminals in the prison. He even sold his hat when he had no food left to give to another prisoner – in the hot sun of Lima a hat was essential. But those whom he loved and pitied most were the men under sentence of death. He stayed with them in their cells, consoling, praying for and with them, preparing them to receive the Sacraments, and to die in the peace of God, by fetching a priest for them. He would accompany them to the place of execution; in some cases he dug their graves when others would have nothing to do with them, alive or dead. In all of those despised and rejected by society Martin saw and loved Christ. Pope Gregory XVI wrote of him that his love for God was so intense that it led him to a truly extraordinary charity towards all his neighbours, so that it embraced all mankind in a truly marvellous way.

Martin was an example of all the virtues, among which his humility was singularly outstanding. His only desire was to serve God through others, seeking no reward or recognition. When the Priory was in financial straits he was saddened to see the superior had decided to sell some of their art treasures. He proposed an alternative solution: why not sell *him* instead? The Negros and many of the Indians and Mulattos were slaves in Peru – there would be no difficulty in finding a buyer – and as he had given himself entirely to serve in any case, this would be a way of doing so. The love and abnegation of his humble Brother made the Prior esteem this *treasure* of the Priory even more and resolve to keep him.

Miracles

Soon reports began to come from various authenticated sources that Martin had the gift of being present wherever he was needed. One day he spent some hours at the home of Juana and her daughter Catalina, having his meal with them and helping to solve a tragic situation which had arisen in the family. Juana was so grateful that she went the next day to thank the Prior for letting her brother visit her. The Prior was very surprised, as he knew Martin had not left the monastery the previous day. To verify this he checked with one of the monks who worked in the infirmary and he too confirmed that Martin had spent those hours working with him attending to the patients.

Martin was embarrassed one day when an African, who had been freed from slavery in his own country, came up to him in the street, knelt and thanked him for the help he had given to himself and his fellow Christians when imprisoned in Africa. Martin tried to make little of it and move on, but the bystanders wanted to hear more. The African then told them that the prisoners were praying together for help when this Brother Martin had come, bringing them food and speaking words of consolation. None of them knew where he had come from, or who he was, until he had met him there in the street in Lima in another Continent. So much admiration and enthusiasm was caused by this event that Martin had to retire to another house of the Order for several months in order to hide himself.

As the years passed, Martin's capacity for work remained undiminished and seemed rather to increase through turning all he did into an offering to God. The flowers he cultivated were for the monastery church; he ensured that medicines would not be lacking by growing the necessary herbs in part of the garden. An olive grove and fruit trees he planted on some waste land were for the use of anyone who passed by. Because of his appreciation of all God's creation, he somehow found time to take care of the animals which people brought to him for treatment; his ability as a vet was remarkable for that time. When visiting the Negro slaves on the farms, taking them what he could, he would feed their animals too. His love extended even to the rats and mice, which he saved from extermination by getting them to move from the monastery to live in a disused outbuilding. One of the witnesses for his beatification testified that Martin had fed a dog, a cat and a mouse together from the same plate.

The external signs of Martin's holiness were the fruit of his hidden life of union with God through prayer, penance, obedience to the Church and devotion to Our Lady – the requirements for every Christian – which he lived to an heroic degree.

When he died on the 3rd of November 1639 he

brought together people of the different races comprising the Peruvian society of his time – Spanish, Creole, Negro, Indian, Mulatto. He died while they were singing the Creed, at the words: *For us men and for our salvation He came down from Heaven; by the Power of the Holy Spirit He became incarnate from the Virgin Mary and was made Man.* Martin made everybody aware of the values which unite the whole human race in mutual love, because all are children of God. At his funeral the Archbishop and the Viceroy carried his coffin; he was surrounded by the prayers of the community and of the crowds who had loved him so much.

Pope John XXIII canonized him on the 6th of May 1962 and his feast is celebrated on the 3rd of November.

THE MARTYRS OF JAPAN

THE STORY OF CHRISTIANITY IN JAPAN

As happened in many other lands previously unknown to Europe, a spirit of adventure linked to a desire for profit from trading was the means of bringing western travellers to the coasts of Japan. The intrepid Portuguese made their way there in the 1540's, and in 1546 a merchant, George Alvares, took on board his ship three Japanese at Kagoshima. Their leader, a man named Anjiro, had killed someone in a fight (it seems to have been accidentally), and was anxious to escape retribution. He was accompanied by two of his servants. Anjiro picked up sufficient Portuguese to be able to communicate with the ship's captain, who as well as being a good seaman was also a good Catholic and lost no time in telling his new friend about his Faith. Anjiro was deeply impressed; for some time he had felt dissatisfied with the Buddhist religion; now he had found the answer to his uncertainty. Alvares told him about a remarkable priest whom he could meet when they reached Malacca (some three thousand miles from Kagoshima) – none other, this remarkable priest, than Saint Francis Xavier.

Saint Francis Xavier

To Anjiro's great disappointment he learned that Saint Francis had left Malacca twelve months previously, but, full of determination, he and his two companions looked for another ship in which to follow him. Anjiro had not been deterred either by the fact that the priest who was in Malacca had refused to baptise him on hearing that the Japanese stranger was intending to return to his Buddhist wife and family. Then followed what seemed to be yet another disaster. The ship was caught in a typhoon which drove it back to the Chinese coast. The three disembarked and met up again with their Portuguese friends. This time they had good news – Saint Francis was due to arrive back in Malacca very shortly. They met him at last and heard him with great interest. The Saint continued instructing the three, during which time Anjiro wrote out the Creed in Japanese; later, having become proficient in the language, he wrote his own life-story in Portuguese. At last Anjiro and his two companions achieved their desire and were baptised by the bishop there on Whit Sunday 1548 – Anjiro was given the baptismal name of Paul, the others of John and Anthony.

With his recent converts to act as interpreters, Saint Francis himself set off for Japan, landing there on the Feast of the Assumption, the 15th of August 1549. They made their way to Kagoshima, where Anjiro immediately told his family and friends about his great discovery of the Catholic Faith, and was instrumental in bringing a hundred or so of his relatives and friends, including his wife and daughter, into the Church. Anjiro remained in Kagoshima while Saint Francis travelled further afield. In the couple of years he spent in Japan – he left in 1551 – there were around three thousand converts. By the the time three decades had passed, the number had reached two hundred thousand, and in 1597 there were over half as many again. The feudal system, which lasted until the nineteenth century, facilitated the spreading of the Faith – if the local rulers were converted, their subjects were also. In 1582 three of these local rulers sent ambassadors to Portugal; these then went on to Rome where they were received in audience by Pope Gregory XIII. They also attended the coronation ceremony of his successor Pope Sixtus V in 1585.

The beginnings of hostility

During the first half-century of Catholicism there was little or no opposition, but gradually the Buddhist leaders began to resent this religion which had come from the West and was making many converts. The missionaries were generally tactful in their dealings with the people, going out of their way to respect their customs and establishing good relations with the authorities, although some mistakes were made in this respect – some rivalries and differences of approach between the missionary orders were apparent, and this did not, of course, help the overall evangelisation. The atmosphere in any case began to get rather strained, although matters were brought to a head purely by accident.

The captain of a trading vessel from Spain dropped the foolish remark that the missionaries were the advance guard of an invasion force from the West. The shogun, Hideyoshi (Taikosama), who until then had been friendly, became hostile. He gave orders for all missionaries to be expelled. Many remained in hiding to continue their work, and on the 15th of February 1597 a violent persecution took place. Twenty-six Catholics were arrested, of whom six were Franciscans, three Jesuits; the seventeen others were Japanese laymen, including a boy of eleven and another of thirteen. They were sentenced to death. In order to terrify any other Catholics and deter would-be converts, the condemned first had part of their left ears cut off and were then paraded around Nagasaki. The two boys were tortured in an attempt to make them deny their Faith. The Japanese Jesuit, Fr Paul Miki, was singled out for harsh treatment because of his apostolic activity; others of his fellow sufferers were John Gotto, a young Japanese aged nineteen; James Kissai, also Japanese, and the first Mexican Saint, the Franciscan missionary Fray Felipe de Jesus.

The blood of martyrs, the seed of Christians...

Paul Miki and the rest were led to a hill near Nagasaki and chained to crosses laid out on the ground, with an iron collar around their necks. The crosses were erected, a soldier with a spear stationed at the foot of each one. The thirteen-year-old started to intone the *Laudate pueri Dominum* which he had learned in his classes of catechism. Paul Miki spoke from his cross encouraging the others, and addressing the bystanders, praying for their conversion. At a given signal, the martyrs were every one of them transfixed simultaneously. The arrest and deportation of missionaries continued; very few managed to remain to continue their work.

In 1598 Taikosama died and the persecution abated for nearly fifteen years. Protestant missionaries arrived in 1609 from England and Holland; these, unfortunately helped to stir up further trouble for the Catholics later on. Things had seemed to be improving, and the ruler of Sendai had even sent another ambassador to the Pope in 1613, but a year later the Emperor Ieyasu Tokugawa issued an edict decreeing the total extermination of Catholicism. The excuse was that he thought the Spaniards were intending to conquer Japan, as they had the Philippines. In 1616 under his successor Hedilada the persecution resembled in its ruthlessness that of the early Christians under Nero and Diocletian. The destruction of the Church was organised systematically; a price was put on the head of every Catholic whether Japanese or foreign; all Japanese were commanded by law to trample on the crucifix every year to show their hatred for Christianity. On the 2nd of September 1622, fifty-two Catholics were killed, twenty-seven of them being beheaded publicly and the remainder burned alive in Nagasaki. Many others were buried alive in various parts of the country. Others were forcibly drowned in the sea, and a few years later thirty-seven thousand of the survivors were put to death in the fortress of Shimobara.

Japan, a closed land

In 1639 a further decree was promulgated forbidding entry to all Europeans. The Dutch traders were the only ones who somehow managed to maintain their right of entry to the ports. The next year, four Portuguese ambassadors were called upon to renounce their Faith; they refused, were tortured and put to death. The remaining Portuguese members of the embassy were sent back to Macao with the warning: *While the sun warms the earth, let no Christian be so bold as to venture into Japan. Let this be known to all men.* Notwithstanding the warning, Spanish missionaries continued to attempt entry. They were one after the other captured and executed after torture between 1642 and 1643. More executions took place in 1647, and this year marked for the Church in Japan the end of all contact with the outside world for over two hundred years. During all the years of persecution the faithful had preserved great devotion to the Rosary, using it as a way of meditating on the life of Our Lord and the Gospels.

Hope re-born

Two long centuries passed with Japan's frontiers firmly closed against all foreigners, until in 1858 a treaty was signed with France for the purposes of trade. In the treaty, one of the conditions laid down by France was that Christianity should be permitted in the ports for the benefit of the visitors. Through the endeavours of the French a church was built in Nagasaki in 1865 at Oura, in honour of the twenty-six martyrs, who were canonized by Pope Pius IX on the 10th of June 1862. The priest in charge was Père Petitjean.

Rumours had circulated that there were still Catholics in Japan, and the French missionaries tried unsuccessfully to locate them. Then, on the 17th of March 1865, when Père Petitjean was in his church, a group of twelve women from the valley of Urakami, about seven miles from Nagasaki, went to the new church and asked the priest to show it to them. When they saw him genuflect before the Blessed Sacrament, they knelt, and one whispered to him, *our hearts – those of all of us here – are the same as yours.* The priest asked where they had come from. They told him, *Urakami. There, all have the same heart as we do.* Then they asked, *Where is Mariasama?* He took them to the altar with the image of Our Lady and the infant Jesus. The women recognised the Baby – Iesusama – and hurried back to tell the others in the village.

The people there had preserved the Faith for over two hundred years, without priests or any of the Sacraments except Baptism. There were at this stage, incredibly, about thirty-thousand Catholics. When the women arrived, hardly anyone believed them; it seemed too good to be true; they also suspected that it could be a trap which could cause further persecution. Little by little, people from Urakami and the islands of

Goto and Kanino went to see the church for themselves. Some fish-sellers, who had been into the city
and made their way to the church, reported back that
they had discovered that the priest there was celibate.
Others went and asked who was his 'head', and
returned saying that it was the Holy Father, the Pope in
Rome. Their fears then receded, and the Church in
Japan, 'in catacombs' for so long, came at last out into
the open. The joy of the Japanese Catholics who now
had priests again was matched by that of the rest of the
Church, especially in Rome. The image of Our Lady
was given the title of *Sancta María de Inventione Chris-
tianorum* – Our Lady of the Finding of the Christians.
The hill outside Nagasaki, with the spring where Baptism was administered secretly for those two long centuries is now known as Mariayama – Mary's Mountain. There is also another hill where the rediscovered
Catholics now set up a large cross. They used to go
there, quietly, as a penance, to pray a long prayer for
reconciliation, which they had learnt by heart, and
which dated back to the seventeenth century. There is
now a bronze relief on the hill where Saints Paul Miki
and his companions died for their Faith, and at the
present day more than half of Japan's Catholics come
from Nagasaki, the city where so many had given their
lives joyfully for Christ.

Their first Japanese bishop was consecrated in
1926, and the feast of the twenty-six Martyrs, on the 6th
of February, at first celebrated only by the Jesuits and
Franciscans, was extended to the universal Church in
1970.

THE MARTYRS OF KOREA

THE STORY OF CHRISTIANITY IN KOREA

One of the more recent feasts included in the Church's calendar is that of the 20th of September – the feast of the Korean Martyrs canonized by Pope John Paul II in a very moving ceremony during his visit to Korea in 1984. He had gone there to commemorate the bicentenary of the Church in that country.

The beginnings – studying the Faith

The way in which the Faith came to Korea is quite unusual. It began with a students' study group. From early in the eighteenth century, interest in Western culture was widespread, and in the 1770's a number of young men whose families belonged to the nobility began to study and discuss books on Catholicism which they had obtained from China. Their original purpose was to compare these new teachings with that of Confucius, as an intellectual exercise, but one or two began to think more deeply about this religion which was so different from anything they knew. One of them was Yi Byok, another Yi Sung Hun (1756-1801), the son of a high court official, a highly intelligent and cultured young man. He could speak Chinese fluently, and could also read and write the language – a feat which few Koreans or other foreigners can emulate. The teachings of Jesus Christ made such a deep impression on him that he tried to put into practice in his own life what he had read, and because of his great enthusiasm several of his brothers and cousins did likewise. Together they studied the beliefs of Catholics for three more years.

The first convert, the first apostle

For Yi Sung Hun the occasion of accompanying his father on a diplomatic mission to China in 1783 was the golden opportunity he had so long desired, of meeting Catholic missionaries in Peking. He stayed for about six weeks, and asked to be baptized. The missionaries examined his knowledge and grasp of the faith and were delighted to be able to grant his wish – he was baptised, receiving the baptismal name of Peter. On his return to Seoul he took with him many books, crucifixes and rosaries. Peter Yi Sung Hun thus became God's instrument for bringing other souls into the Church. The first one he baptized was his friend Yi Byok – from then on known as Jean-Baptiste. Shortly afterwards came the Chong brothers, the Kwon brothers and then a whole stream of converts. One of them, Kim Bom-u, gave his house to be used as the first Catholic church in his country. A hundred years later the Cathedral of Seoul was erected on the same site.

The new converts met every Sunday to pray and study their faith. They abandoned the rigid class-distinction prevalent in their society, and ceased offering sacrifices to their ancestors (a custom of the Confucian religion). They addressed each other as 'believer-friend', and carried out a very effective apostolate of spreading doctrine by distributing Catholic writings which they had translated into Korean. On considering the spread of the Church there, one realises more and more how important it is for Catholics of all walks of life to read and study the teachings of the Church, both to preserve their own faith in the face of difficulties and to be able to transmit its doctrine to others.

The numbers of converts increased rapidly over the following years, during which they pleaded with the bishop of Peking to send priests. These wonderful apostles of the faith had received so far only the sacrament of Baptism.

Official opposition

The spread of the new religion had not passed unnoticed in official circles, and in 1786 a ban was put on all Christian publications – the enemies of the Church understanding perfectly well the power of the written and printed word. In 1789 Kim Bom-u, the donor of the first church, was arrested, tortured and put to death. Further complications arose two years later when the mother of Paul Yun Chich'ung died and was buried by her family according to the Catholic rite. Paul and his brother-in-law James Kwon Sang Yon did not carry out the Confucian sacrifice or burn the wooden tablet inscribed with the deceased's name, which was an important part of the ancestor worship. As Paul and James were of noble families, news of this not surprisingly reached the Emperor, Chong-ho. It was absolutely unheard of for any noble to reject the worship of his ancestors; it was interpreted as a lack of respect for parents, and hence an act of disloyalty to the monarch. Paul Yun Chich'ung and James Kwon Sang Yon were therefore executed on the 7th of December.

The persecutions continued; the Catholics reiterated their appeals for priests, and in 1794 a Chinese priest, Fr Chou Wen-mo (1752-1801) was sent by the bishop of Peking. He reached Seoul in 1795, finding to his amazement and joy that there were about four thousand Catholics for him to look after. For the first time these faithful Catholics were able to attend Holy Mass and receive all the Sacraments. It is perhaps difficult for us to imagine their situation, when we have such marvellous opportunities for practising our faith. It does make one realise, however, the need to pray that we may never take for granted the great treasure we have, and instead take seriously the encouragement we are given to pray for many more priestly vocations.

Fr Chou worked assiduously among his Catholic flock and also made many converts; he managed to escape arrest for six years, and by the time he was caught in 1801 his charges numbered around ten thousand. In that year the Emperor Ching-ho was succeeded by his daughter, who, like her mother the Dowager-Empress, hated Christianity and organised a violent persecution. A five-household mutual- guarantee system was set up – an organised spying network, enabling the rapid discovery of all Catholics, immediately followed by their arrest. Three hundred Catholics were killed that year, including Fr Chou and Peter Yi Sung Hun (b.1756) *the first convert*, who had been baptized in Peking; his uncle, Yi Kakwan (1752-1801), and members of the original study group formed in 1777. They included the elder brother of the distinguished scholar Chong Yagong – he himself was banished together with his younger brother, who was a Catholic.

Those who survived fled to the mountains to take refuge wherever they could. An appeal for help was sent to the Catholic authorities in Peking. The message, painted on a long piece of silk with over thirteen thousand characters, was dated 21st October 1801. In it the author Hwang Sayong describes the persecutions. Unfortunately the message was intercepted; Hwang Sayong was captured and became yet another martyr for his Faith.

Perseverance in the face of trials

The situation lasted for almost another thirty years – the faithful were still without priests, yet each year more and more people were converted, knowing that they were risking their lives by doing so. A few Catholics managed to reach Peking and plead again for priests – they even appealed to Pope Pius VII, informing him that there were now at least ten thousand Catholics in Korea.

In 1815 and 1827 the persecution intensified in its savagery – and the number of Catholics increased rather than diminished. Later there was some respite when the Andong Kim clan came to power, since the head of the clan, Kim Chosun, was himself a convert. Taking advantage of the improvement, an Apostolic Vicariate was set up for Korea, and the long-awaited priests set off for their new country. Initially there were two, both of them French, Fr Pierre-Philippe Maubant (1803-1839) and Fr Barthelemy Brugiére, who sadly died on the way. Two more priests then joined Fr Maubant in 1837 – Fr Jacques Honoré Chastan and Fr Laurent Joseph Marie Imbert. The Korean authorities were overjoyed, but their period of calm was short-lived. Persecution again broke out after the death of Kim Chosun and a hundred and thirty people were martyred, including the three French priests in 1839.

In 1845 a new Vicar Apostolic arrived accompanied by two other priests, one of them Fr André Kim Taegon (b.1822), the first Korean priest, who had now returned after studying in the seminary of Macao.

One year later, in 1846, all three were executed.

The fruits of fidelity

By the 1850's the Catholics had increased to around twenty-three thousand. The Andong Kim clan regained power at this time, providing a further period of peace. A seminary was started at Chech-on, and the converts continued to multiply.

However, due to another dynastic change in 1864 when a child-emperor came to the throne, with his father acting as regent, the toll of martyrs soared up into the thousands. The rulers considered that the economic difficulties of the country were the result of foreign contacts, and in the attempt to remove all traces of influence from abroad the Church was again the main target for attack. Four hundred Catholics were killed in Seoul alone, and in 1868 upwards of two thousand more; a further eight thousand odd were either killed or sent to forced labour in 1870.

The Catholics of Korea have suffered some of the worst persecutions in the history of the Church, even until relatively recent times, and yet they have kept the Faith, preferring it to their own lives and transmitting it from generation to generation, just as they themselves received it.

Their faith, fortitude and perseverance has been rewarded. At the beginning of the century there were about fifty thousand Catholics; they now exceed two million, with the highest proportion of baptisms and conversions in the universal Church.

THE MARTYRS OF UGANDA

The African interior had waited many centuries for the coming of Christianity, and it was not until the late 1800's that missionaries from various European countries followed in the footsteps of explorers like Dr Livingstone. Portugal, Spain, Italy and France took the Catholic Faith to the areas they colonised, whilst Holland and England also spread Protestantism. Around 1880 a group of White Fathers were sent by Cardinal Lavigerie from Algeria, which was under French rule, to Buganda in East Africa, a part of what is now Uganda. The travelling conditions were appalling; they made the journey from Zanzibar on foot, a journey which cost some of the missionaries their lives, and others their health. Those who reached Buganda after several months of trekking through the jungle found the situation far from encouraging.

19th Century Buganda

The country was governed by an absolute ruler (the Kabaka), who at that time was a man called Mukabya; he was also known as Mutesa I. The people were considered as his property; women in particular had no rights; everyone was expected to act always in accordance with the wishes of the King. His behaviour was somewhat reminiscent of that of some of the early and less reputable Roman emperors – Caligula, Claudius, Nero – whose viciousness held human life and dignity as of no value except insofar as his people could be compelled to satisfy his every whim. The missionaries quickly pointed out to Mukabya the error of his ways, reminding him of the dignity of every human being. Mukabya was infuriated. No-one had ever dared to correct him. He responded by expelling the missionaries, who withdrew across the border. Later they were able to return.

These were times of political upheaval, however, and Mukabya found his country surrounded by opposing forces – the Moslem Egyptians in the North, the French and English rapidly advancing from the East and South. Realising that he could not hope to drive off all these enemies, the Kabaka planned to set one faction against the other. He tried to enlist the aid of the French by recalling their expelled missionaries, telling them to make their government intervene on his behalf by sending him troops. The priests explained that the purpose of their coming was purely spiritual. They could not get involved in politics. A good deal of the success these priests achieved was the result of their faithfulness to their role as priests, obeying the Church in all that they did and making themselves available to all souls without exception – and all this in the face of the anger of an all-powerful monarch. Mukabya then turned for assistance to the Moslems, whose intervention suited his purpose in more ways than one. Apart from military reinforcements, he was given encouragement for his corrupt life-style by his new allies.

Charles Lwanga

In 1882, after the missionaries had been at work in Buganda for about three years, the Kabaka's rage was again turned against them, so the few converts either fled the country or remained to practise their faith in hiding, contriving to meet secretly to pray together. A number of these were itinerant tax-collectors whose work involved travelling to the different villages under the Kabaka's rule. These men formed with their connection of routes throughout the country the only link between the missionaries and the scattered Christians or prospective converts. At this time a young Bugandan called Lwanga held an important post with one of the local chieftains. As one of his duties he had to attend the Kabaka's emissaries on their visits. Through them he came into contact with Catholics for the first time. One day on entering the hut where the messengers had been lodged Lwanga found the men kneeling. He asked them what they were doing, and they told him: *praying*. This puzzled him as there was plainly no idol for them to pray to. They explained that they were praying to God, who is a spirit and is invisible; they also described to him in brief terms the coming of the Son of God made man in order to redeem mankind. From then on Lwanga joined them to pray on each of their visits, and to receive from them further instruction. Then someone informed the chieftain that his visitors were Catholics. Lwanga interceded for them and to his surprise the chieftain, who had a great respect for his young helper, encouraged him to continue learning about Christianity and also to learn how to read and write. For three more years his life followed the same pattern, his knowledge and love for the Faith growing all the time.

The new Kabaka

1885 brought relief and new hope to the people when news came of the death of Mukabya. He was succeeded by his son, Mwanga, who showed interest in the opportunities for education brought by the Europeans to his country. The missionaries were very happy when invited to return and asked to set up schools. Mwanga even promised to appoint Christians to important positions in his kingdom as a pledge of his good will. Some time previously Lwanga had been nominated as one of the attendants at the royal court. He was a talented young man, known for his loyal and efficient service to the chieftain. He was also skilled as a wrestler. The task given him at the court was to take charge of all the royal pages. Mwanga was as good as his word and chose three Catholics for influential posts, Joseph Musaka Balikuddembe, who became a member of the King's Council, Matthias Kalumba Mulumba, and Andrew Kaggwe, who became a chieftain. The future for the Church seemed secure.

As Mwanga consolidated his control over the country it became more and more obvious to all that he had certain traits of character very much in common with his father – a propensity, for example, to violent outbursts of uncontrollable anger – and, much worse, an inherited tendency to vice. Lwanga realised that it was going to be vital to keep the young pages away from the Kabaka, and providentially the Kabaka himself supplied the opportunity. He wanted the pages to prepare a park and lake for his use, and therefore had authorised their being absent from the court. Meanwhile Lwanga's desire for baptism and love for his faith persuaded the missionaries to waive the usual rule of a four-year preparation period, and he was baptized on the 15th of November 1885 by Fr Giraud, receiving the name of Charles. This policy of making would-be converts wait for so long was to prevent anyone becoming a Christian for the wrong motive – hope of material gain, for instance, or in order to receive a good education etc. They had to be prudent, therefore, as there were now many who expressed the wish to become Catholics.

Trouble brewing

The Kabaka oscillated rather unpredictably between anger at the Christians and seeming to favour them, even at one point allowing the royal audience hall to be used for classes for the pages, whose teachers were Charles Lwanga, who taught the boys, and Joseph Musaka, who looked after the young men. These two not only instructed their charges in the duties of their office as pages, but also introduced them to the precepts of the natural law and Christian morality and doctrine. This enabled the pages to support and encourage each other in living an upright life in the corrupt atmosphere of the court. Needless to say, their attitude progressively angered Mwanga.

In the same year, 1885, a German occupation of the coast seemed imminent. The Kabaka began to distrust all Europeans, and his pagan counsellors made use of the opportunity to sow suspicion in his mind concerning the Christians in his kingdom, insinuating that they were plotting his overthrow. That the missionaries and converts were aware of danger is shown by what Fr Lourdel told twenty-two Ugandans whom he baptised on the 1st of November, the feast of All Saints. His statement that they might not see the same feast day again proved to be prophetic.

Joseph Musaka, first Ugandan martyr for the Catholic Faith

Mwanga in his fury decided to punish the Catholics in his court, accusing them of disloyalty because they would not obey him in behaviour that they knew, and he refused to admit, was immoral. Joseph Musaka was summoned on November the 14th; his 'trial' lasted throughout the night. On the following morning, the capricious ruler allowed Joseph to go. He immediately went to the mission centre where his first act was to attend Holy Mass and to receive Holy Communion. While he was warning the missionaries of the situation at court a messenger arrived – he was to return at once to the Kabaka. The latter was again in a frenzied rage. "Musaka", he stormed, "you are condemned to be burnt as soon as the fire can be lighted."

Then I am condemned for my faith, was the reply.

Joseph was imprisoned, the guards allowing no-one to visit him. As the missionaries heard nothing after Joseph's hurried departure, they became more and more concerned. Fr Lourdel set off for the palace. He was not allowed to see Joseph, or to have an audience with the King. He sent the Kabaka a message pleading with him not to harm an innocent person. Mwanga hesitated, but when Joseph was brought before him with all the courtiers assembled, like Herod he lacked the courage of his convictions. Afraid of losing face if he released his prisoner, he ordered the guards to take him out and execute him. When they went to tie him he told them not to worry, because he would not try to escape. *A Christian who loves God is not afraid to die,* he said. Escorted by the guards he walked calmly to the place of execution. The chief executioner, who had great admiration for Joseph, could not bring himself to make him die the slow, agonising death by fire, so he asked for a sword. Joseph knelt and was beheaded. His body was thrown into the fire. The date was the 15th of November 1885.

The aftermath

Mwanga thought that by having one of his chief counsellors put to death for the Christian faith he would ensure that no-one else would dare remain Christian in his domain. He was proved wrong. As soon as news of Joseph Musaka's death reached the people, twenty of the royal pages went to the mission and asked to be baptized, fully aware that by doing so they were placing their own lives in jeopardy. The missionaries completed the instruction of the boys and the young men, baptized them and gave them their First Holy Communion. Among this group were James Buzabaliawo and Bruno Serunkuma, who later died martyrs. The newly-baptized pages returned to their duties and were soon able to profess their faith before the Kabaka, who called them all together, ordering all those who prayed to admit it by coming forward. All except three did so. Mwanga and his council could hardly believe their eyes. So many Christians in the royal court! Beside himself with fury, Mwanga shouted that unless they renounced their religion and ceased praying, he would have them all slaughtered. He would not tolerate Christianity, because it sought to impose a moral law even on the King – he was not prepared to accept that!

The result of his outburst was that a further forty pages went to ask for Baptism. These were followed by numerous adults, deeply impressed by the faith and courage of the young people. The missionaries intensified the classes of instruction. In his fit of hatred and rage, Mwanga dismissed all Christians from official posts at court, Charles Lwanga being the last to remain. Again there is a similarity between this cruel king and Herod, who often went to converse with his prisoner John the Baptist, fascinated yet fearful, and finally putting to death the very man who could have helped him. Mwanga constantly asked Charles questions, then attempted to undermine his faith, trying to turn him against Christ because *Jesus was a white man.* To this Charles replied that God was not concerned about the colour of a person's skin, but about the state of his soul. For a while longer, the Kabaka allowed Charles to continue his classes with the pages, but all the time they were aware that the storm clouds were gathering. Various political problems preoccupied the Kabaka, whilst his pagan followers redoubled their efforts to turn him once more against the Christians, whose high moral standards stood out as a sign of their beliefs – as happened among the early Christians.

The storm breaks

Two relatively insignificant incidents brought matters to a climax. One was on the 22nd of May 1886, when a visitor of notorious ill- repute came to spend some time as a guest at the court. A banquet was given in his honour and he requested a particular page to attend him. The boy refused, realising that in doing so he would draw down the Kabaka's anger on himself, but preferred to risk punishment rather than act against his conscience. This time, however, Mwanga said nothing; but he did not forget. Shortly afterwards, the king returned earlier than expected after leaving the palace. Some of the pages were not there to greet him. They were with Charles, learning about the Catholic Faith. This was the last straw for the Kabaka, even though Charles was able to assure him that everything was in order. He condemned the Christians to be executed. Charles immediately told the young ones to run for their lives; they replied that it would be like denying their faith. A message was sent to the mission centre. The pages were all thrown into prison on the 25th May. Orders were given for wood to be collected for the fires.

The last days

Charles had now put himself at their head and encouraged his companions. Some of them reminded him that they had not yet been baptized. He gave them a final class and baptized them himself in the prison. Among them was Nbaga, the son of the chief executioner. They prayed all night together. The following morning, May the 26th, a declaration was issued to the effect that Christianity was prohibited. Anyone who prayed would be considered a criminal and dealt with accordingly. Christians were branded as traitors.

Fr Lourdel hurried to intercede, offering his own life for that of the pages. Mwanga refused and ordered him to leave. The pages were called and commanded to prostrate themselves before the king, get up, and stand in his presence. He then said that those who still wished to pray should go to the other end of the room. The entire group went, with the addition of a boy who stepped out of the crowd of onlookers. Then a guard threw down his spear and joined them. Fr Lourdel again intervened. But Mwanga was adamant. The pagan counsellors, fearing their king might relent, kept pressing him and asked for the arrest of Andrew Kaggwe, a tribal chief. (Through Andrew's apostolate most of the people of his area had become Catholic.) He was arrested and put to death. Three died in jail under torture; another, a young boy called Gonzaga Gonza died on the death march to Namugongo.

People were summoned from all the villages to witness the executions, which were carried out in the hope of finally driving Christianity from the country. Further arrests were made, the victims being mutilated but not killed. The Kabaka was still determined that the rest of the pages should die.

Fr Lourdel, the other missionaries, and Bishop

Livinhac, the Vicar Apostolic recently arrived in the country, did all they could to obtain the release of the remaining prisoners. The pages, fastened in stocks, prayed the Rosary together. On the 3rd of June 1886 they were led along with their hands bound to where the fires had been got ready. The bystanders were amazed at the courage and serenity of the youths; one young boy started to cry, but refused to leave his companions. Charles consoled and encouraged him. Fr Lourdel gave them his last blessing as they passed by. Later he wrote to Cardinal Lavigerie: *Charles Lwanga led them with a look of determination on his face, with great serenity and interior peace.*

The crown of martyrdom

On reaching Namugongo the prisoners thanked God for the perseverance of the whole group. Charles was then selected to be killed first. The fire was made to burn slowly so as to prolong his agony, during which he uttered no protest. Just before dying he called upon the name of God. The rest were then offered their lives if they renounced their faith. Not one of them accepted. Each was then rolled in a reed mat, placed among the branches which were already prepared, and set on fire. They prayed aloud until they died. Among those forced to be witnesses of the execution were some Catholic children, who not only encouraged the martyrs but even offered to die with them.

Far from extinguishing the faith, the deaths of the martyrs led to many more conversions and strengthened those who were already Christian. Some heroic non-Catholics had also given their lives rather than obey the Kabaka. The remaining Christians had to go into hiding for a while, and further executions took place, the last being that of Jean-Marie Muzeyi, who was beheaded.

Beatification and canonization

In 1920 Pope Benedict XV beatified the martyrs. At this very moving ceremony three men were present who had been among the children witnessing the martyrs' death, and who could have been among the victims of the Kabaka but had lived and passed on the faith. The Holy Father received them in audience, and people in the crowds at St Peter's went forward to kiss their hands.

Pope Paul VI canonized them in 1965, setting their feast day for the 3rd of June.

The life and death of these recent converts show how the grace received through the sacraments gives strength to overcome all obstacles and dangers. Most of them were quite young, some mere boys, yet they had the courage to resist the immoral practices of the time. They understood very clearly that there can be no true promotion of man's dignity unless the essential order of his nature is respected.

The martyrs of Uganda show that by corresponding with God's grace everyone can live a fully Christian life in any circumstances.

SAINT MAXIMILIAN KOLBE

Raymond Kolbe was born on the 8th of January 1894, the second son of a weaver at Zdunska Wola near the city of Lodz in Poland. As is traditional in that country, the family had great devotion to Our Lady, which became part of life for the children. Like most small boys, Raymond was frequently in trouble for the usual childish misdemeanours, until one day when his parents saw that he had changed. At the time he said nothing; the explanation emerged only later. He related that after being reprimanded by his mother, that night he had asked the Blessed Virgin what was going to happen to him. Our Lady then came and offered him two crowns, one red, the other white, asking if he would be willing to accept either of them. She told him that the white crown represented purity, the red, martyrdom. Raymond said he would accept both. A dream? A vision?... From then on, the boy felt prepared for a martyr's death.

When he was thirteen Raymond went with his elder brother to the junior seminary of Lwow, run by the Franciscans. His keen interest and ability in mathematics and science and any type of military activity made his teachers come to the conclusion that he would choose a career as a scientist or strategist. For a time he dreamed of being a soldier, to fight for the freedom of his country, losing interest in the original plan of becoming a priest. In 1910, however, he asked to enter the Franciscan novitiate, receiving his new name Maximilian when given the habit. He was selected to go to Rome to continue his studies, first philosophy, from 1912 to 1915 in the Gregorian university, then theology to 1919 in the faculty of Saint Bonaventure. Whilst in Rome, with six of his companions he founded the Crusade of Mary Immaculate – *Militia Immaculatae* – with the purpose of *converting sinners, heretics and schismatics, particularly freemasons, and bringing all men to love Mary Immaculate*.

Devotion to Our Lady

The day of his priestly ordination came on the 28th of April 1918. By the time he returned to Poland in 1919 he was suffering from tuberculosis, which the doctors told him was incurable, one lung being out of action and the other damaged. His poor health did not prevent him from working intensely to spread his Crusade of devotion to Our Lady, whose feast as Queen of Poland had recently been instituted by Pope Pius XI. He combined his work of teaching theology with his Marian apostolate, and in 1922 launched a publication, 'Knight of the Immaculate', first in Cracow, then in Grodno, where he set up a small press.

Soon the volume of work exceeded the capacity of the publishing works, so in 1927 further possibilities were sought. The answer to prayer came with an offer of land in Teresin. The first 'stone' to be laid was a statue of Our Lady, and the friars began to build. On the 8th December 1927 the new friary was consecrated and named Niepokalanow, City of the Immaculate, a centre for disseminating devotion to the Mother of God. The small beginnings developed rapidly. Soon there was a junior seminary for missionary priests, and the whole enterprise grew to the proportions of a small town with over seven hundred inhabitants – brothers, priests, seminarians – who exercised various professions, making the project completely self-supporting. Other publications followed the 'Knight of the Immaculate', and recognition of the value of this apostolate came from the hierarchy, who wrote to the Holy See stating that it had helped the people to withstand the horrors they endured during the war.

Once the seminary, the printing press and everything in Niepokalanow was making progress, Fr Maximilian turned his sights to other lands which he could win over for Our Lady. With a special blessing from Pope Pius XI he set off with four companions in 1930 for Japan, arriving in Nagasaki in April. When asked where he would find the necessary finances, he replied, *Money? It will turn up somehow or other; Mary will see to it; it's her business and her Son's.* The Archbishop was delighted to receive the missionaries, and Fr Maximilian was asked to occupy the post of lecturer in philosophy in the diocesan seminary. He would also have the use of printing facilities for his magazine. The first Japanese edition was printed a month after their arrival. Within a year they had obtained land on Mount Hikosan on the outskirts of the city, where the 'Garden of the Immaculate' – *Mugenzai no Sono* – was to be built. (Due to its location the place survived the atomic attack which would later devastate the greater part of the city.) Only external obstacles prevented Fr Maximilian from setting up similar establishments in Korea, China and India, and he even travelled to Moscow, studying the possibility of publishing his magazine in Russian.

Imprisonment

In 1936 he returned to Poland; by then his health had deteriorated considerably, his condition being aggravated by his inability to adapt to Japanese food, and yet he continued to work without respite. Three years later, in September 1939, the 'City of the Imma-culate' was overrun by the occupying troops and the priests, brothers and seminarians were deported to Germany. They were allowed to return on the 8th of December, the Feast of the Immaculate Conception. Fr Maximilian then dedicated all his energies to helping the thousands of refugees, many of whom were Jews fleeing from persecution. Naturally this activity attracted the attention of the Nazis.

After the 1941 edition of their publication, Fr Max-imilian was arrested on the 17th of February and sent to the dreaded Pawiak prison in Warsaw. Ill-treatment soon followed. A witness described how one of the guards approached him – he was still wearing his Fran-ciscan habit – and asked if he believed in Christ. Fr Maximilian replied, *Yes, I do*, whereupon the guard struck him. The question was repeated again and again, always receiving the same reply. The priest was beaten viciously. After this incident he was deprived of his habit and had to wear the prison uniform.

On the 28th of May together with three hundred others he was sent to Auschwitz concentration camp. He was branded as prisoner 16670. Everyone wore the conspicuous striped convicts' uniform. The work was extremely hard, moving planks and stone blocks, the prisoners being forced to run while carrying their bur-dens. One of the guards conceived a special hatred for Fr Maximilian and let pass no opportunity of treating him harshly. When the priest collapsed from exhaus-tion, the guard beat him and had him flogged until he seemed to be dead. His companions managed to carry him to the hospital block, where he remained for some days in great pain. Even so, he dedicated himself to hearing confessions and speaking to the other prisoners of the love of God. Frequently he would stand back when food was distributed, allowing others to go first, or he would share his meagre portion with someone else. Fr Maximilian gave peace and hope to those around him. His calm demeanour and self-forgetfulness, despite the inhuman treatment, made a deep impression on the other inmates. He continued his priestly work, administering the Sacrament of Penance to many.

One day, at the end of July 1941, the camp sirens were sounded, indicating that some prisoners had escaped. The rest were all driven from the huts to line up before the officers. When the numbers had been checked, it was discovered that three men had gone, one from one of the huts, two from another. The camp commandant ordered that ten prisoners from those huts should be sent to the underground death cell to die by starvation. The ten were picked at random from the rows of prisoners. An eye-witness then recalled that he saw another prisoner go forward to speak to the commandant, who showed great surprise at what was said. An order was given. One of the ten men was sent back to his group, and the other prisoner – Fr Maximilian – took his place in the line which filed silently into the death bunker.

No greater love ...

Fr Maximilian had heard the man whose place he had taken cry out in despair, *My poor wife and children, I shall never see them again.* He had then offered his life in exchange for the other; the Nazi officer had accepted his offer. Further details came from the interpreter in the condemned cells. He told the tribunal for the cause of beatification that each day Fr Maximilian led prayers and hymns among his companions, who were joined by men in the other cells. When the guards opened the cell doors to inspect the men, the prisoners begged for food, but were pushed back roughly, some actually being shot.

As the days dragged on and the strength of the dying men failed, they could pray only in whispers. Fr Maximilian helped each of them, as one by one they died. He was always found kneeling or standing, looking serenely at the guards whenever they inspected the cell. At the end of two weeks, he was the sole survivor. The interpreter gave an account of his last day. The guards had become impatient. They needed the cell for more prisoners. They sent for one of the medical staff, who approached the priest with a hypodermic syringe. Fr Maximilian held out his arm himself to be injected with carbolic acid, which caused excruciating pain. At that point the interpreter went away, unable to watch what was happening. He returned later and found Fr Maximilian sitting against the wall, his head bowed to one side, his eyes open and his face calm and radiant.

News of his heroic death travelled swiftly through the camp, spreading hope and faith among the prisoners. The report of his sanctity was carried to other camps and elsewhere. In the midst of the turmoil and brutality Fr Maximilian had been a shining example of the love of God and heroic charity for others, overcoming hatred and evil with his goodness.

Requests for his beatification resulted in the cause being introduced very soon after his death. Pope Paul VI declared him *Blessed* in 1971, and on his historic visit to Poland, Pope John Paul II prayed in the cell where the holy priest gave his life. The Pope from Poland canonized the Polish martyr priest on the 10th of October 1982. His feast is on the 14th of August, the eve of one of the great feasts of Our Lady, whom he loved and served so well.

Saint Nicholas of Bari

Very little is known of the lives of numerous saints of the early Church, among whom is Saint Nicholas, whose feast is on the 6th of December. In some countries, small children believe that he is the *Santa Claus* who brings them gifts on that day. The earliest *Life* of the saint dates from the ninth century and records oral tradition; it became the source for other later biographies. Methodius, Patriarch of Constantinople, wrote a short document on him around the year 842, and by the thirteenth century a narrative recounting many pious and wonderful deeds of Saint Nicholas was in circulation.

He is thought to have lived in Myra, near Patara in the province of Lycia (now part of Turkey), in Asia Minor. His birth was probably around 270, his death somewhere between 345 and 352. In spite of the scarcity of detail concerning his life and person, the fact of his sanctity is undeniable. He is venerated from early in the fifth century as a Bishop and *Thaumaturgos* – wonder-worker – by both the Greek and Latin rites. By about 430 a church in his honour had been built by the Emperor Justinian in Constantinople; four other churches in the same city also had him as a Patron. According to some Greek sources, Saint Nicholas suffered imprisonment under the persecution of Diocletian, making an eloquent defence of his faith. He is also said by some to have attended the Council of Nicea in 325, called to refute the errors of Arianism. His name, however, is not included in the list of those taking part in the Council.

Many marvellous works were attributed to him, even during his lifetime; from infancy he is said to have fasted on Wednesdays and Fridays; he somehow produced gold for the dowries of three young girls too poor to marry; he is said to have restored to life three little boys killed by an innkeeper who put their corpses in a large barrel. On other occasions he miraculously saved the city from famine and rescued sailors from shipwreck. He refuted idolaters and converted many Jews and Arabs. After his death, miracles through his intercession continued whenever he was invoked.

How his relics came from their resting-place in the cathedral of Myra to the Church of Saint Stephen at Bari, in Italy, is a somewhat unorthodox testimony to the great esteem in which Saint Nicholas was held in the West. In 1087 a group of sailors from the port of Bari, where there were many Greek immigrants, set off on an expedition to Myra, aided and abetted by two priests, to bring back the relics of the saint. A similar plan had been made in Venice, but the sailors from Bari arrived first. They entered the Cathedral, opened the tomb and removed the relics, making their escape safely to the ship and bringing Saint Nicholas to honourable burial in their own home port. Again, many miracles took place at his new tomb, and through his intercession. The motive for the expedition was not only the pious desire of keeping the relics in Christian hands – the Moslems by that time had many strongholds in Asia Minor – but ensuring that the prestige of their city was considerably enhanced by the possession of the relics of such a popular saint. Since that time, many churches in the West have been dedicated in his honour. In various places he is still the Patron of sailors, and of children, and is credited with a willingness to help in solving what seem to be impossible financial problems.

Saints Perpetua and Felicity

The spreading of the Christian faith in the first centuries was facilitated to a great extent by the organisation of the Roman Empire, which dominated, pacified and gave its culture to many nations. Communication was also made easy by the common languages Latin and Greek. The earliest persecutions of the Church were also an effect of the policies of this same Empire. Official religious practice was part of civic duty. Those who refused to participate were regarded as atheist, disloyal to the Empire and hence dangerous. Worship of Rome and of the Emperor, who embodied the authority and dignity of the State, was a normal part of life. Polytheism was general and Rome had no objection to incorporating the deities of conquered nations, expecting these nations to correspond by rendering divine honour to the ruler.

The Jewish nation, and later the Christians, were misunderstood and frequently misrepresented. In the reign of Nero Christians were officially blamed for the burning of Rome which caused enduring resentment among the people; the Christian faith was considered *a pernicious superstition, depraved and extravagant*, by writers such as Tacitus and Pliny the Younger; Christians were even believed to practise infanticide and cannibalism. In any civil disturbance the Christians were usually held to be the culprits. Since their religion was declared to be *an unlawful superstition*, the mere fact of being a believer was a criminal offence.

To become a Christian meant undertaking a life of doubtful security and was highly dangerous in those

times when the cult of the Emperor and the gods was
enforced as a means of fortifying the position of the
ruler and of establishing law and order. Edicts were
then promulgated, such as that of Septimius Severus in
201, forbidding conversions to Christianity. Thanks to
the efficient system of communications and administrative government, the effects of the edict were felt very
soon in Carthage, the centre of a flourishing Christian
community in North Africa.

Tertullian and Saint Augustine give several quota-
tions from the *Acts* of some of the Carthaginian martyrs
who gave their lives in 203 AD rather than deny their
faith. Part of the narrative referring to events before
their martyrdom was written by Saint Perpetua, another
by the deacon Saturus, one of her companions in
suffering, and the account of their death was added by
one who was an eye-witness. This *Passio Perpetuae et
Felicitatis* was probably written originally in Latin and
then translated into Greek, both versions having been
widely circulated among the Christians of Carthage.

At the beginning of the third century the proconsu-
lar province of Africa was governed by the procurator
Hilarion as the proconsul had died. When the edict of
the Emperor was enforced, five catechumens were
arrested – three men, Revocatus, Secundulus and
Saturninus, and two women. Vibia Perpetua aged
twenty-two, was of noble family, married and with a very
young child; the other, Felicity, a slave, was in an
advanced state of pregnancy. Shortly after they were
detained, Saturus, the deacon who had instructed them
in the faith, surrendered voluntarily to aid his catechumens and was imprisoned with them. Perpetua's mother
and one brother were Christian, another brother was a
catechumen and the youngest had died as a child. Her
father was pagan. Her narrative relates how they were

at first kept under guard at a private house where attempts were made to persuade them to give up the faith. The most severe trial for Perpetua was the pleading of her father; apart from his affection for his only daughter, her being a Christian seemed to him a disgrace upon the family. When he could not dissuade his daughter by arguments, he beat her in his anger.

It was after this episode that Saturus administered Baptism to the five. They were then all transferred to the public prison – of which Perpetua writes, *I was shocked at the horror and darkness of the place, for till then I knew not what such sort of places were.* The prison was overcrowded and unbearably hot; they were illtreated by the guards, and in addition Perpetua was very concerned about her child. Two other intrepid deacons bribed the warders to allow these prisoners to be moved to a part of the prison where conditions were slightly better; the baby was brought to Perpetua, who was able to feed him. She then handed the child over to her mother and says she was *much afflicted to see the concern of her mother and brother* for her.

Whilst awaiting trial Perpetua had a vision in which her martyrdom was announced as well as that of Saturus, who was to be the first to die. When the date of their trial was made public, her father came again to the prison, distraught with grief. He appealed to her with all his heart, as only a father could: *Daughter, have pity on my grey hairs, have compassion on your father – if I myself have brought you up to this age, if you consider how my extreme love of you made me always prefer you to all your brothers, make me not a reproach to mankind. Have respect for your mother and your aunt; have compassion on your child that cannot survive you, lay aside this resolution, this obstinacy, lest you ruin us all: for not one of us will dare open his lips any more if this misfortune befall you.* Perpetua relates that he took her by the hands at the same time, and kissed them; he threw himself at her feet in tears and called her no longer daughter, but, 'my lady'. She adds how much she suffered on his account, knowing that he did not understand.

They were sent to trial the following day; a large crowd gathered to watch the proceedings. The Procurator Hilarion acted as judge. All of them when questioned declared that they were Christian... Perpetua's father appeared, with her baby, again beseeching her to change her mind; even the judge Hilarion used the same arguments, appealing to her affection for her father and her child, commanding her yet again to offer sacrifice to the Emperor. Perpetua refused, acknowledging that she was a Christian, whereupon her father tried to pull her with him to safety. He was beaten back by order of the Procurator. Sentence was given. The five were to be exposed in the circus to wild beasts. (Secundulus had already died from his treatment in prison.) The men, Revocatus, Saturninus and Saturus, were flogged, and Perpetua and Felicity were beaten about the face. The sentence was to be carried out on the festival celebrated for Geta, a son of the Emperor, who had been made Caesar four years previously.

One of the first fruits of the steadfast faith and fortitude of these Christians was the behaviour of their prison officer, Pudens, who treated them as well as he was able and allowed visitors to come freely. On the day appointed for the games in honour of Geta, Perpetua's father made a final effort to save his daughter; in her words, *'He tore his beard, threw himself prostrate on the ground, cursed his years and said enough to move any creature; and I was ready to die with sorrow to see my father in so deplorable a condition.'* Despite her great anguish for one whom she loved so much, by God's grace Perpetua was enabled to remain faithful.

She received further visions, as did Saturus, relating to their future happiness in Heaven through the sacrifice of their lives. The account of their last hours is continued by the witness, who gave details also of the valour of Felicity, the chief cause of whose distress was that, as she was pregnant, she could not be executed until after the birth of her child, and would probably not therefore be able to accompany the others. Even though Roman law permitted great cruelty in dealing with those who were considered criminals or enemies of the State, the innocent lives of unborn children were protected. Felicity and her companions prayed that the child would be born prematurely – it was in its eighth month by that time – and their prayers were granted. She gave birth in the prison, shortly before they were to be killed, and when one of the guards heard her cry out in pain he asked how she would react when thrown to the animals. Felicity answered, *It is I that suffer what I now suffer; but then there will be Another in me that will suffer for me because I shall suffer for Him.* The baby, a girl, was taken into the family of one of the Christians who visited them.

The martyrs were treated with severity during their last days, being deprived of food, and for a while visitors were forbidden. When Perpetua spoke to the tribune he relented, and the warden Pudens did what he could to alleviate their suffering; by this time he too had become a Christian. When they were led into the amphitheatre an attempt was made to dress them according to the pagan custom, the men as priests of Saturn in red cloaks, the two women as priestesses of Ceres. On their objecting that they had been promised they would not be coerced into doing anything contrary to their religion, they were allowed to go dressed as they were. The people demanded that they should be scourged, so they were made to pass in front of soldiers who each lashed them with a whip.

Like the Apostles, they rejoiced *that they had been found worthy to suffer indignity for the sake of Jesus' name* (Acts 5:41). A bear, a leopard and a boar were set against the men. Saturus was mortally wounded by the leopard, and before dying encouraged Pudens the prison officer to persevere in his faith. Perpetua and Felicity were attacked by a wild cow. Perpetua was the first to be tossed. After her fall, realising that her garments were torn, she immediately gathered her tunic about her, caring more for her modesty than about the injuries she had received. She then got to her feet and fixed back her hair which had fallen loose, not wanting to present a dishevelled appearance like that of one in mourning. Felicity had been badly wounded by the cow and Perpetua assisted her to stand. Both awaited the next charge of the animal, but even the crowd at this stage took pity on them and called for them to be given the *coup de grâce*. Perpetua had the opportunity of exhorting her brother and the deacon Rusticus to remain faithful, then the four survivors were led out to be executed by swordsmen; Perpetua was wounded several times before the fatal blow.

Veneration of these martyrs was widespread in the early Christian Church, particularly in Carthage. A basilica was later erected over their tomb and Saint Augustine preached there on several occasions. Their feast was fixed for the 7th of March, the day of their martyrdom, their names being thereafter included in the Roman Canon of the Mass.

POPE SAINT PIUS X

The young priest

The second son of Giovanni Battista Sarto and his wife Margherita was born on the 2nd of June 1835 in Riese, a little village in Lombardy. Their first son had died shortly after birth, so Bepi, as he was called, became the eldest of their family of eight. The boy was very quick at learning and the curate of the parish took it upon himself to teach him Latin. When Bepi was eleven he attended the nearest grammar school, which was in Castelfranco, four miles away. As money was scarce he had to make the journey on foot, at times carrying his shoes so that they would last longer. His final examination results were outstanding. He had spoken to the parish priest of his desire to become a priest himself; his parents, despite their poverty, were delighted that their eldest son had this vocation and placed no obstacles in his path. In 1850 he was given a scholarship to study in the seminary of Padua. He was ordained priest in the cathedral of Castelfranco on 18th September 1858 and went as curate to Fr Antonio Castantini in Tombolo. The parish priest took good care of the formation of his curate and began to have a very high opinion of him. Writing to a friend he said, *They have sent me a young priest with orders for me to form him to the duties of a parish priest, but I assure you that it is likely to be the other way about. He is so zealous, so full of good sense and other precious gifts that I could learn much from him.* He commented that his new curate would not share his cloak with a beggar – he would be more likely to give him the whole

garment! The people of Tombolo were impressed by
the striking recollection with which he celebrated the
Holy Mass and by his concern for souls. He spent many
hours hearing Confessions, teaching and preaching.
Requests for his services as a preacher began to come
in from neighbouring parishes. As curate he received
very little income, most of which he distributed among
his poorer parishioners. When taken to task by Fr
Antonio, who told him he should save something for his
mother, he said simply, *These poor people are in greater
need than she; Our Lord will provide for her also.* Most
of the work of the parish fell on Fr Giuseppe for
several years as Fr Antonio suffered from very poor
health.

When in 1867 Fr Giuseppe was transferred to Sal-
zano as parish priest, his previous parishioners were
inconsolable; his new flock were somewhat surprised
that their new parish priest had come from such a small
village, but soon learned to value his holiness and his
concern for them. As parish priest he insisted constantly on the importance of teaching catechism to children and adults in order to counteract the widespread
ignorance of the doctrine of the Church. His solicitude
for the poor was proverbial; during an outbreak of
cholera he visited the sick, administered the Sacraments, attended the funerals which took place at night
through fear of contagion, and even helped to carry the
coffins and dig the graves. This total dedication to his
work with souls did not prevent him from studying; he
stayed up at night. In this way he acquired a profound
knowledge of Sacred Scripture, the *Summa Theologiae*
of Saint Thomas Aquinas, and Canon Law.

In 1875 the Bishop of Treviso summoned him to
be a canon of the Cathedral, Spiritual Director of the
Seminary and Chancellor of the Diocese. He undertook

the formation of the future priests with great zeal, in addition to his administrative work, which was increased by the death of the Bishop, as he was then required to act as Administrator of the diocese until the appointment of a successor.

The Bishop's task

One day in 1884 the new Bishop invited him to his private oratory, suggesting that they should pray about something which concerned them both. He later communicated to Monsignor Sarto that the Holy Father, Pope Leo XIII, had appointed him Bishop of Mantua. Considering himself totally unworthy of this dignity, Monsignor Sarto wrote to the Pope asking him to choose someone more suitable – to no avail. He was ordained Bishop on the 16th of November 1884 and went to his diocese early in the following year. The diocese was in a state of disarray; lack of knowledge of the Christian faith was rife, political differences had caused rivalry and division, and many of the priests were no longer fulfilling their pastoral duties. Firmly and gently the Bishop guided all his flock back to the Church. The priests he won over by making them aware of their duties and working in close cooperation with them. Everyone found a kindly welcome at the Bishop's house. The story is told of a young priest calling there early one morning to ask permission to do some research in the archives; he had just celebrated his Mass in the Cathedral. It was the Bishop himself who opened the door and, realizing the priest would not have had breakfast, took him along to the kitchen to prepare something for him. The priest, Fr Achille Ratti, was the future Pope Pius XI.

Formation for his people

One of Bishop Sarto's first concerns was to re-establish the seminary which had been closed for the previous ten years. Soon there were almost a hundred and fifty students. The doctrinal formation of everyone, priests and laity, was again being given attention in a practical way. His pastoral letter of 12th October 1885 emphasized the need for teaching the catechism. For this purpose a catechetical school was set up in each parish; children were to be instructed every Sunday, as were adults through regular preaching on the mysteries of the Faith, especially during Lent and Advent. There had been no diocesan synod for two centuries; Bishop Sarto convoked one in 1888 to study in depth the problems to be tackled and plan the measures that would have to be taken. When for some reason there was no priest available to teach catechism in one of the parishes, the Bishop performed this duty himself, also dedicating many hours each week to hearing confessions. Through his efforts the people were taught the traditional Gregorian music, enabling them to participate more fully in the solemn liturgy.

Pope Leo XIII, who had for some time been following closely the work being carried out by Bishop Sarto, created him Cardinal in 1893. The Bishop resisted, at first but accepted the decision of the Holy Father. That same year he was made Patriarch of Venice. He was prevented from occupying the See by the anti-clerical government of the Republic, which claimed the right to nominate the Patriarch and consequently refused to recognise the appointment of Cardinal Sarto. In the meantime he returned to Mantua, also making a visit to his birthplace, Riese, where he was accorded a rapturous welcome. His mother was by this time confined to her house; her son went to her wearing the robes and insignia of Cardinal. (His father had died when he was in the seminary.) Pressure on the civil authorities by the people of Venice compelled them reluctantly to accept the Cardinal, who reached the city on the 24th of November 1893, acclaimed by all except the members of the government. Cardinal Sarto took the initiative in trying to establish better relations with the secular administration, writing to the Mayor expressing his desire for them to work in cooperation. His concerns were, as in Mantua, the instruction of the people and the formation of the clergy. He reformed the seminary there in accordance with the decrees of the Council of Trent; one of his pastoral letters showed how religious ignorance brought with it the lack of appreciation and eventual loss of the Faith. He paid special attention to the pastoral care of his priests so as to foster their piety and interior life. Long retreats were organised so that, as far as possible, they could attend one each year, and every month there was a day of recollection, which the Cardinal himself frequently preached, gathering his priests around him to pray. Courses of theology, biblical exegesis, etc. were given, to reinforce and intensify their knowledge of doctrine.

Cardinal Sarto's personal life of poverty continued as before. The entire staff looking after him consisted of two of his sisters and a niece. Meals at the patriarchal palace were simple; whatever money was available went to remedy the needs of the poor; when there was nothing else, his watch went to the pawnshop to provide the few lire somebody needed.

The anti-catholic policy of the civil authorities had taken firm hold in many areas of Venetian life. Crucifixes had been removed from the schools, processions and outward manifestations of piety had been banned. The Cardinal continually reminded his faithful of their civic duties, of, for example, their right to vote; in the 1895 elections the municipal council chosen no longer included the anti-catholic elements it had previously contained.

His sorrow was indescribable when sacrilege was committed in the Carmelite church in his Diocese. The ciborium containing the Blessed Sacrament was stolen and the Sacred Hosts scattered along the street. In his desire to atone for this outrage, he arranged a Eucharistic Congress for Venice in August 1897. The ceremonies were held with the greatest possible splendour and were attended by Cardinals, Bishops, priests and thousands of the faithful. The lasting effects of the Congress were an increase in Eucharistic devotion which surpassed all expectations.

Roman Pontiff

After a pontificate of twenty-five years, Pope Leo XIII died on the 20th of July 1903. The conclave to elect his successor started on the 31st of that month in the Sistine Chapel. During the proceedings the Austrian Cardinal Puzyna delivered the veto of the Emperor of Austria against Cardinal Rampolla, Secretary of State of Leo XIII. The Secretary of the Conclave, Monsignor Rafael Merry del Val, was sent to persuade Cardinal Sarto not to continue in his refusal to be elected Pontiff, as he had besought the other Cardinals not to vote for him. Monsignor Merry del Val found him praying before the Blessed Sacrament and delivered his message. With tears running down his cheeks he asked the Monsignor to ask them not to think of him. At the seventh ballot, Cardinal Sarto was elected to the See of Peter, fully aware of the heavy cross he was being asked to shoulder. In a low voice he said, *If this chalice may not pass away but I must drink it, Thy Will be done.* When asked by what name he wished to be known, he answered that as the Popes who had suffered most for the Church in recent times had all been called Pius, he too would take that name.

As Roman Pontiff, one of his first acts was to revise the system of papal elections, eliminating all possible interference by abolishing the right of veto. He nominated Monsignor Merry del Val, a Prelate of Spanish descent who had studied in the English seminary of Ushaw, as his Secretary of State, later creating him Cardinal. This Cardinal remained faithfully by the side of Pius X, providing unfailing support in all the difficulties the Pope encountered. In his first encyclical, *E supremi apostolatus cathedra*, after paying tribute to his predecessor, Pius X pointed out the main cause of the evils besetting society at that time – the widespread apostasy from God; man setting himself up in opposition to and in the place of God. He announced the motto for his pontificate – *Instaurare omnia in Christo* – to restore all things in Christ, calling upon his Bishops to *form Christ in those who are destined by the duty of their vocation to form Him in others. We refer to priests,* he said. Reminders were given about the care to be taken over seminaries and over young priests recently ordained; *Enkindle them and inspire them so that they may aspire only after God and the salvation of souls.* A warning was given against the fallacious ideas which lead to rationalism. The Pope stated very accurately that it is not true that progress in knowledge extinguishes faith; it is ignorance that does it. The more ignorance prevails, the greater is the havoc wrought by lack of belief. He then exhorted the clergy and faithful to play their part diligently in making the true doctrine of Christ known, starting from a basis of prayer.

Audiences with the Holy Father were thrown open

to all the people. Apart from the more formal private ones for diplomats etc., each Sunday Saint Pius X received large groups from the parishes of Rome, preaching to them on the gospels and giving catechism classes to the children in the Cortile di San Damaso. He reduced the number of attendants who accompanied him and simplified some of the complex Vatican protocol, thereby giving the people easier access to their Pastor. Ever aware of the needs of a growing city, he reorganised the Rome Vicariate, setting up more parishes in the suburbs.

An enormous task which he engaged in was the revision of the Code of Canon Law, initiated on the feast of Saint Joseph, the 19th of March 1904; five years later he streamlined the Roman Curia, reducing the administrative processes and outlining clearly the competence of the various departments, minimizing the duplication of work caused by overlapping between the departments, and thus rendering them far more effective.

1904 also saw the issue of the encyclical *Ad diem illud*, to mark and celebrate the golden jubilee of the declaration of the dogma of the Immaculate Conception of Our Lady. The Holy Father called upon Christians to have recourse to Mary in order to reach Jesus; *Recourse to Mary*, he said, *is the surest and easiest means for uniting all persons with Christ and obtaining through Him the perfect adoption of sons.* He stated very clearly the role Our Lady was chosen to play in the plan of the Redemption: *Since Divine Providence willed that the God-Man should come to us through Mary, who conceived Him through the Holy Spirit and bore Him in her womb, we can now receive Christ only through Mary.* One of the chief ways Saint Pius envisaged as a means of restoring all things in Christ was by an increase in devotion to the Mother of God throughout the world.

In his encyclical to mark the thirteenth centenary of Saint Gregory the Great, the Pope brought to mind some of the basic truths of the Faith which were falling into oblivion. *If you destroy the principle that there is a Divinity beyond this visible world, nothing is more evident than that unbridled passions of the lowest and vilest kind will be unleashed and that minds enslaved by them will run riot amidst disorders of every imaginable kind... Nor will civil authority ever be able to prevent these or other evils as long as it forgets or denies that all authority comes from God... Take away God, and all respect for civil law disappears. Take away God, and justice is spurned, and the liberty that arises from the natural law is trodden underfoot. Take away God, and men will destroy the very structure of the family, the primary and indispensable foundation of the whole social structure.* As a remedy the Pope goes on to stress the need for prayer and the teaching of the truth, a prerequisite being *the principles of a true and solid philosophy and theology*, and, even more important, ensuring that the moral teaching of Christ be in the minds and hearts of all. Speaking of charity, he warns against the danger of a false *'charity'* which sacrifices true doctrine in a mistaken attempt to win over those who are in error, adulterating the teachings of the Church and thinking that by so doing they make these more palatable: *Truth is one; it cannot be divided. It remains forever, free from the vicissitudes of time; 'Jesus Christ is the same, yesterday, and today, yes, and forever'.*

Opposition

Anti-clerical governments in several countries caused severe trials for the Church and great suffering to the Holy Father. In Germany, Spain and Portugal there were many difficulties, even resulting, in Portugal, in the persecution of the clergy. The situation in France was even more acute. The combined efforts of the atheist government in alliance with the Freemasons were aimed at a separation of the Church and the State, seizure of Church property and interference by the government in religious affairs. The way had been paved by the proposal of laws forbidding religious education in schools, by the re-establishment of divorce in civil law and by the denial of the right of religious orders to teach. Clerics were no longer to be exempt from military service, and dismissal was demanded for officers of the armed forces or of the Civil Services if they practised their Faith. Saint Pius denounced these proposals in a letter to the President; the reply was a severing of diplomatic relations with the Vatican and the immediate enactment of the laws against members of religious orders and decreeing the separation of Church and State. Other letters from the Pope followed, protesting in strong terms against the obvious injustices and illegal declarations, including the unilateral rescinding of the Concordat. The Pope rejected the subsidy offered by the French government in exchange for the State's control of the Church. All Church property was at once requisitioned; priests, bishops and religious were left homeless and without income. The result was not what the government had expected. The Catholics of France rallied round the Pope and his representatives in their country; the impoverished Church gained much in an increase of fervour and a closer union with Rome.

Modernism

An even heavier cross than the attacks of anti-

Christian forces was the insidious poison spreading from within the ranks of the Catholic clergy, mainly from lecturers and students from some seminaries, who were trying to *modernize* the Church, to bring it in line with modern philosophical thought, adapting it to the times in which they lived. A new *creed* was to be produced, considered more in accordance with the discoveries of science; faith was subjected to current ways of *analytical* thinking, instead of bringing God's light and truth to mankind. There was no organized system in Modernism, as this series of errors came to be called. It was an attitude which permeated the whole of the outlook of those affected, reducing the supernatural to the purely natural. The errors were diffused rapidly, from within the hierarchy through priests and teaching establishments. The promoters of the new ideas wrote against Church doctrine, some using several different names.

Condemnation of some Modernist theories had been pronounced when in 1903 works by Loisy and Houton had been included in the Index, and also in *Iucunda sane*, the encyclical issued for the anniversary of Pope Saint Gregory. The Archbishop of Paris received a letter from the Pope showing Loisy's intractable disposition despite his protests of orthodoxy; the Italian hierarchy were put on their guard against this 'Modernism' which the Pope had described as the compendium of all heresies. The decree *Lamentabili sane* of the 3rd of July 1907 condemned sixty-five propositions from the works of Loisy, Blondel, Tyrrel and Le Roy, of which twenty-eight had already been censured as being Protestant in their foundation. The decree was the first methodical exposition of Modernist teaching, and showed the extent to which this was in opposition to and undermined the basic tenets of the Faith. The self-styled *Catholic intellectuals* infected by Modernist ideas attacked the divine inspiration of Holy Scripture, which they insisted on treating just like any other ancient text, submitting it to a purely human interpretation. Catholic teaching was said to be irreconcilable with the origins of Christianity and contrary to history. They claimed independence from the Magisterium in determining the sense of the Sacred writings and in denying the veracity and historicity of the Gospels. From there, the Modernists moved on to deny the divinity of Jesus Christ, and made a distinction between *the Christ of history* and *the Christ of faith*. The virgin birth, the Redeeming death and Resurrection of the Saviour were also rejected. Then there were the Sacraments: these were considered to have originated with the Apostles and their followers to remind man of the presence of the Creator – none of them, said the Modernists, was instituted by Christ. The priesthood evolved gradually, they would have it, from those who customarily presided over the *supper*. Finally, as to the Church: they flatly declared that Christ had no intention of founding a Church which would continue throughout the centuries, since He thought the coming of the kingdom and the end of the world were imminent. Peter *never even suspected that Christ entrusted the primacy in the Church to him*(55). *Truth is no more immutable than man himself, since it evolved with him, in him and through him* (58). The final proposition summarized the rest: *Modern Catholicism could be reconciled with true science only if it was transformed into a non-dogmatic Christianity; that is to say, into a broad and liberal Protestantism*(65).

The decree, as might have been expected, raised considerable opposition from Modernist circles supported by the press. This did not deter the Pontiff from publishing on the 8th of September his exposition of the roots of those errors, and of the characteristics of the underlying philosophies, in the long encyclical *Pascendi dominici gregis*, which ends with practical measures for stemming the heresy. The extreme gravity of this trend, arising as it did from within the Church and reaching all aspects of her life, the astuteness and audacity of the propagators who *played the double part of rationalist and Catholic*, called for immediate action. The encyclical was a last resort on the part of the Pope, who had tried encouragement and private correction of the individuals, but without success. An analysis of the philosophies shows how the Modernists move from an initial agnosticism to historic atheism, leaving God aside in their explanations of the history of the human race. Religion then becomes the product of a subconscious sense of the divine, a purely subjective phenomenon; all religions in the light of this are equally valid. Science for the Modernists was to be completely independent of faith, but at the same time faith was made subject to science. Their theology, based on immanentism, came in some cases very close to pantheism, and through their belief that everything is subject to change through evolution, the permanent nature of the faith and dogma of the Church was denied. The Modernists were eager to reform the philosophy and theology taught in seminaries, manifestations of devotion were to be reduced, and ecclesiastical government was to be completely revised. Some, following Protestant guidance, demanded the suppression of priestly celibacy. Great efforts were made by these people to ridicule and undermine the Magisterium of the Church, the authority and tradition of the Fathers, and the Scholastic method of philosophy, recognizing in these the bastions of orthodox Catholicism.

The importance of a sound philosophy

After calling for vigilance on the part of bishops, educators and superiors, and urging them to detect and deal firmly with any deviations, the Holy Father outlined his plan of remedies, starting with philosophical studies. *We will, and strictly ordain, that scholastic philosophy be made the basis of the sacred sciences ... let it be understood that We understand chiefly that which the Angelic Doctor (Saint Thomas Aquinas) has bequeathed to us. We admonish professors to bear in mind that they cannot set aside Saint Thomas without grave disadvantage.* More recent Popes have also indicated the importance of the teachings of Saint Thomas as a basis for sound Catholic theology. Bishops are then told of their responsibility in ensuring that no writings harmful to the Faith should be tolerated in the seminaries or centres of education under their jurisdiction. Nor should they grant the Imprimatur lightly; Catholic booksellers have a grave responsibility not to sell publications contrary to the Faith. In 1914 the 'motu proprio' *Doctoris Angelici* insisted again on the value of Saint Thomas' works and, to curtail the spread of Modernism, an oath against its errors was to be taken by all lecturers and teachers, together with a profession of faith. Clerics and religious were also to abide by the contents of the oath. These exhortations and warnings of Saint Pius X made Catholics aware of the dangers in their midst; unfortunately many of the Modernists refused to heed the Pope, continuing to publish their theories, the effects of which are still causing harm within the Church.

Mindful of the need of priests who were holy, learned and entirely dedicated to the service of God and of souls, he addressed himself to the clergy on the 4th of August 1908, the fiftieth year of his priesthood.

Already in his first encyclical he had emphasized the importance of priestly formation; he had arranged for an apostolic visitation of all the Italian seminaries, promoting the setting up of regional seminaries instead of having one in each diocese in those areas where the number of candidates was very small, or qualified teaching staff was lacking. The plan of studies was revised. Priests were called once more to a life of authentic sanctity, vital to those who were called to act *in nomine et in Persona Christi*. He set out a programme of pastoral activities for the good of souls, and of virtues which every priest should strive to acquire; Saint John Vianney is named as an example. Speaking of prayer, the Pope said, *there is a necessary union between prayer and holiness, so that one cannot be had without the other.* A fixed time each day was to be set aside by priests for this, which would be the remedy against the danger of routine in carrying out their sacred duties, and provide a protection from becoming worldly. Warning was given against activism, with the consequent neglect of interior life; the Pope showed the apostolic sterility of such an attitude – human talents cannot be substituted for the priest's union with God, from which all efficacy with souls is derived.

The Pope's efforts to foster an authentic Christian life among the faithful, as he had done in his earlier years, was marked by his insistence on the urgent need for teaching doctrine. In *Acerbo nimis* after explaining how the will is moved to action by the intellect and a Christian way of life follows on from the knowledge of doctrine, he quotes Pope Benedict XIV: *There is nothing more effective than catechetical instruction to spread the glory of God and to secure the salvation of souls.* Part of this instruction was to prepare children for the reception of the Sacraments of Penance, Confirmation and Holy Eucharist. Adults were not to be neglected either, and parish priests were instructed to prepare a cycle of sermons based on the Catechism of Trent. Bishops were to ensure that all this was done satisfactorily in their diocese.

The Holy Eucharist

Perhaps Saint Pius X is best remembered as *the Pope of the Blessed Sacrament*. In 1905 he reminded the faithful of the indication of the Council of Trent recommending the reception of Holy Communion by the faithful in each Mass, which meant daily. Frequent reception of the Holy Eucharist was the way to nourish the spiritual life and would be *the antidote whereby we may be freed from daily faults and be preserved from mortal sins*. To counteract the lingering traces of Jansenism, still apparent in many areas, the Pope says of Holy Communion that its primary purpose is not *that it may serve as a reward bestowed on the recipients, or as a recompense for virtue*. Because of Jansenist rigorism, many people went to Communion only once a year, and *whole classes of persons were excluded from a frequent approach to the Holy Table – for instance, merchants or those who were married*. The controversy as to who should be allowed to communicate was finally settled by this decree. All the faithful (including children) of any condition, provided they were in a state of grace, had a right intention and observed the prescribed fast, could go frequently, even daily, to Holy Communion. A *right intention* is defined and the decree states that, although it is fitting that the recipients should be free from venial sin, (at least deliberate ones), it is however sufficient that they be free from mortal sins with the purpose of avoiding these sins in the future. It is also pointed out that, whilst the Sacraments always produce their effect *ex opere operato*, the good dispositions of the faithful favour a greater effect from the Sacrament, hence the care that should be taken in preparation beforehand, and in thanksgiving afterwards.

Finally, children, who at that time were not permitted to receive Holy Communion until they were twelve or fourteen (many even died without having received Our Lord), were to make their first Holy Communion once they had attained the use of reason. *The age of discretion, both for Confession and for Holy Communion, is the time when a child begins to reason, that is, about the seventh year, more or less.* From then on begins the obligation of fulfilling the precept both of Confession and Communion. A full and perfect knowledge of Christian doctrine is not necessary for either First Confession or First Communion. Afterwards there is an obligation for the child to learn the whole catechism gradually. *The knowledge of religion which is required in a child in order to be properly prepared to receive First Communion is such that he will understand according to his capacity those Mysteries of faith which are necessary as a means of salvation (necessitate medii), that he can distinguish between the Bread of the Eucharist and ordinary, material bread, and thus may receive Holy Communion with a devotion becoming to his years.* A practical illustration of this teaching was given by Saint Pius during a private audience with an Englishwoman accompanied by her small son. After observing the little boy the Pope called him over, asking his age. He was four. The Pope then asked him, *Whom do we receive in Holy Communion?* The boy replied, *Jesus Christ* – and, *Who is Jesus Christ?* – *Jesus Christ is God.* Turning to the mother, Saint Pius told her to bring the child the following day and he would give him his First Communion.

As had happened in Venice as a result of the Eucharistic Congress, so all over the world devotion to the Blessed Sacrament increased. Many letters of gratitude were sent to the Vatican by people of all walks of life and, in 1912, from France – the country where the Church had suffered so much – came a pilgrimage of four hundred First Communicants, representing the children of France, to express their thanks to the Holy Father personally.

The final years of the Pope's life were overshadowed by the impending tragedy of World War I. He foresaw the outcome of the assassination of Archduke Ferdinand of Austria in June 1914, calling this *the spark that will start the blaze.* On the 2nd of August he addressed an exhortation to the Catholics of the world, asking them to turn back to the One who alone can give peace.

On the 20th of August he died, aged eighty, attended by his faithful companion, Cardinal Merry del Val. Recognition of his sanctity was immediate and worldwide. The cause for his beatification was initiated in 1923, but was delayed by the Second World War; in 1951 Pope Pius XII beatified him and canonized him three years later. Saint Pius X is the first Pope to be proclaimed a saint since Saint Pius V, who died in 1572. His feast is now celebrated on the 21st of August. (Until 1969 it was on the 3rd of September.)

SAINT ROSE OF LIMA

Whilst the Protestant Reformation was causing great harm to the Catholic Church right across Europe, the countries on the other side of the Atlantic were opening up an immense field of apostolate. Priests had gone there with the first *conquistadores*, bringing the Faith to the natives of those lands. As time passed, more priests and religious left their own shores to work in the New World.

Towards the end of the sixteenth century in Peru there were settled areas with already several generations of Catholics. The family of Saint Rose was among these. Her father, Gaspar de Flores, originally came from Puerto Rico and her mother, Maria Oliva, was from Lima. Rose was born on the 20th of April 1586, and at her baptism was called Isabel after her maternal grandmother. Very soon her family began to call her *Rose* – some authors say because of her beauty, which could easily be true judging from a portrait of her painted in 1617, the year of her death, by Angelino Medoro. It is now kept in the shrine dedicated to Saint Rose and shows that indeed she was exceptionally lovely. When she was confirmed she took Rose as her name; the Archbishop who performed the ceremony was Saint Turibius of Mongrovejo, the same holy Prelate who had also confirmed the other Saint from Peru, Martin de Porres.

Rose was one of a large family of twelve, and spent much of her time helping her mother with the younger children. The family were not particularly wealthy, but endeavoured to give their children, including the daughters, the best education available. Rose grew up a cultured, artistic young woman, well-known among the educated society of Lima.

Life of prayer and penance

From quite an early age Rose had developed a strong and deep interior life through prayer and mortification. She prayed for several hours each day and practised severe penances and long fasts. When she was still only a girl she made a vow of perpetual virginity. Her family would not consent to her joining a religious order, although one of her brothers had become an Augustinian, but on the 10th of August 1606 she joined the Third Order of Saint Dominic, taking the name Rose of Santa Maria. There was no convent of Dominican nuns in the area, so women could belong only to the Third Order. In this way Rose continued to help in her family and at the same time to receive spiritual guidance for her soul.

As her model Rose took another great Saint of the Third Order, Saint Catherine of Siena, who also lived a life of intense prayer and sacrifice. Sometimes during her prayer Rose was seen to be in ecstasy, especially when in the presence of the Blessed Sacrament. When she could be alone she remained in contemplation for long periods of time. Many people, attracted by her reputation for holiness and by her welcoming attitude, went to visit her asking for her prayers and advice, which always helped them to seek union with God in their own lives.

Rose prayed a great deal about the Passion of Our Lord and longed to accompany and console him in some way. She wore an ornamental silver band around her hair which had many small spikes on the inside pressing on her head to resemble his Crown of Thorns;

she carried a rough chain around her waist and used to put bitter herbs into her food. She also passed through long periods of spiritual aridity and a feeling of being abandoned by God which caused her more pain than all the physical sufferings she chose to inflict upon herself out of love for Christ and for sinners.

The other Christian virtues were also very much part of her life – because she constantly struggled to acquire them and improve in them, with the result that she was a very affectionate, attractive character. Not content with taking care of her own immediate family, she looked after numerous sick people, especially those who were poor. She even set up a small hospital beside their house. Children too were the object of her special attention. She loved to be with them, teaching them and helping to form them. For her they were the hope of the future, potential apostles who in their turn would bring souls to Christ.

For the last three years of her life Rose went to stay with some friends, the family of Gonzalo de la Maza and his wife, as they needed assistance. During this time, she suffered several grave illnesses and, when in pain, was heard to say, *Lord, increase my sufferings and with them increase Thy love in my heart.* She died on the 24th of August 1617, aged thirty-one. Although the greater part of her life was spent in obscurity, at her death crowds came to venerate her even then as a Saint. Her funeral was attended by the Archbishop, representatives of the civil authorities and many of the townspeople. Her first resting place was in the cloister of the Dominican monastery; her remains were then moved to the church of Saint Dominic to give easier access for all who wished to pray near her. Miracles through her intercession multiplied, and in 1668 she was beatified by Pope Clement IX, who in 1669 named her as Patron of Lima and of Peru. In 1670, the same Pope declared her Patron of America and the Philippines.

In 1672 he canonized her – the first American to be proclaimed a Saint. Devotion to her continues to spread and her feast is now held on the 23rd of August. Her burial place is in the same chapel as that of Saint Martin de Porres in the Convent of the Rosary in Lima.

SAINT THOMAS AQUINAS

Thomas, the youngest son of the house of Aquino, was born probably towards the end of 1225 in the castle of Roccasecca near Monte Cassino, in the kingdom of Sicily. Count Landulf, his father, was a nephew of the Emperor Frederick Barbarossa and was also related to Pope Gregory the Great, Saint Louis King of France, and King Ferdinand of Castile. His mother was a descendant of the Norman Barons who had conquered Sicily two centuries earlier.

When Thomas was five he was sent to school at the famous Benedictine monastery of Monte Cassino. Little is known of his early years, apart from one or two events. When very small, being cared for with his young sister by their nurse, the latter were both killed by lightning during a storm. The baby Thomas survived. For the rest of his life he had a great fear of thunderstorms, and would usually be found, during them, in the church, near the tabernacle. In school, one of the monks who found him deep in thought, asked him what he was thinking about. He received the reply *Tell me, what is God?* – a question he spent his whole life studying.

The Dominicans. Family opposition to his vocation

By the time Thomas was ten he was sent to the University of Naples to continue his studies. Emperor Frederick II had commandeered the monastery of Monte Cassino as a fortress and expelled the monks and their pupils. As a consequence, he was excommunicated by Pope Gregory IX. It was in Naples that Thomas first met the Order of Preachers, whose founder Saint Dominic had died some twenty years earlier. The Dominicans were mendicant friars who dedicated themselves to prayer, study and preaching. Thomas felt that his vocation was within this Order and spoke to one of the Friars, John of Saint Julian.

At the age of sixteen he was admitted and given the habit. As Thomas had expected, his widowed mother, the Countess Theodora, who had cherished hopes of seeing him as Abbot of the great Benedictine monastery, objected strongly to her son's becoming a friar, reduced to begging for his living. When Thomas went to the Dominican monastery of Santa Sabina in Rome, his mother followed, hoping to dissuade him from his decision. The General of the Order, John of Wildeshausen, was about to travel to Paris and decided to take Thomas with him. Countess Theodora then commanded her two sons Landulf and Raymond, who were serving in the army of the Emperor, to detain their young brother and take him back to Roccasecca. The small group of friars was ambushed, Thomas was seized and forcibly taken back to the castle. The soldiers had attempted to drag his habit off him but eventually gave up when Thomas unexpectedly resisted with determination. Back at the castle his mother and sisters Marietta and Theodora tried all manner of persuasion, and finally his mother in exasperation had him imprisoned in one of the towers of the castle. Through his example and conversation, Thomas won his sisters over to understand his desire to serve God. Marietta later saw her own vocation as a Benedictine nun; Theodora married the Count of San Severino and became an excellent wife and mother.

Through the help of these sisters Thomas was able to obtain books and writing materials to continue his

studies. He persevered in his vocation against all opposition for over a year, until in 1245 he was able to
escape, aided by his sisters, and was let down the castle
wall in a basket to a group of Dominicans who took
him to Naples. His mother was still determined to
make him leave the Order and appealed personally to
the Pope. Thomas was sent for and appeared before
the Holy Father who, having listened to Thomas, was
firmly convinced that his vocation was from God and
forbade the family to interfere any further.

In the universities

In 1247 he was sent to continue his studies at the
University of Paris, where he met the Franciscan Saint
Bonaventure, who like Saint Thomas was to be given
the title of Doctor of the Church. Both obtained their
University degrees in 1248. Shortly afterwards he went
to Cologne University under the Dominican Saint
Albert the Great. Some of his fellow students jokingly
called Thomas *the dumb ox*, partly on account of his
stature and also because, in the disputations, Thomas
listened in silence, giving no hint of his outstanding
intelligence. One of his companions kindly offered to
explain the lectures to him. Thomas humbly accepted
with gratitude. On one occasion this student-teacher of
his had not understood a particularly difficult problem
and was astonished when Thomas proceeded to give a
profound and lucid explanation. Saint Albert was aware
of Thomas' genius and also of the fact that the other
students had little appreciation of this, so, in their presence, he questioned Thomas on various difficult
matters, receiving replies which revealed to all of them
the wonderful talents Thomas possessed. Saint Albert
then commented to his students, *You call Brother Thomas the dumb ox, but I tell you he will one day make his*

bellowing heard to the uttermost parts of the earth.

After four years of study in Cologne Thomas was ordained. Under the guidance of Saint Albert he now began teaching in the University. Four years later he again went to Paris, this time to receive his Doctorate. His lectures at the Priory of Saint James attracted so many that the halls were filled to more than capacity. Recognising his ability, the University authorities, although Thomas was ten years younger than the qualifying age according to the statutes, allowed him to begin his Doctor's degree course. It was at this time, around 1252, that Thomas produced some of his philosophical writings – *De Ente et Essentia, De Principiis Naturae*, and part of his *Commentary on the Sententia of Peter Lombard.*

Disturbances arose in the University from the opposition of some secular Doctors to the Dominicans and Franciscans, wishing to prevent these from retaining their posts as lecturers. A pamphlet attacking the Religious was produced; the King, Saint Louis IX, referred the publication to the judgment of the Holy See. Saint Thomas and Saint Bonaventure were sent to Rome as representatives of their respective Orders. They defended their cause admirably and the University was obliged to re-admit the friars to their chairs of theology. In 1256 both Saint Thomas and Saint Bonaventure received the degree of Doctor. Whilst continuing his lecturing at the University, Saint Thomas preached frequently and, at the command of the Superior of the Order, Saint Raymond of Peñafort, wrote some of his commentaries on the Bible, on Boethius' *De Trinitate*, and part of the *Summa contra Gentiles*. This was to combat the false philosophical and theological ideas introduced by the Moors into Spain and thence into the European universities. He was at the same time acting as counsellor to the French king, Saint Louis. It is said that sometimes, when absorbed with some particular topic, Saint Thomas was oblivious to what was happening around him. On one of the occasions when he was dining with the King, Saint Thomas suddenly struck the table with his fist exclaiming, *That's the end of the Manichees!* His companions tried to remind him where he was, but the King just sent for a secretary to take down the argument Thomas had developed against the heresy.

Philosopher and theologian

In 1259 he returned to Italy and was appointed theological adviser to the Pope and professor of the schools attached to the papal court. This meant he had to spend some time in Anagni, Orvieto, Rome and Viterbo. The volume of his written work increased considerably during this period. He always preceded his studies by intense prayer and never neglected his priestly pastoral work. He wrote commentaries on the philosophical writings of Aristotle, using the Greek texts. Previously, Aristotle had been viewed with suspicion by Christians, as his works had been made known through mistranslations of Arab scholars. Saint Thomas recognised the validity of Aristotle's thought, and in his writings always refers to him as *the Philosopher*. Making use of Aristotle's philosophy, Saint Thomas demonstrated the harmony between reason and faith, showing how a knowledge of the existence of God can be attained by reason from the created world, and how the implications of dogmas of faith could be expressed in precise terms, making philosophy truly the *ancilla Theologiae* (the handmaid of theology), with no opposition between truth, as known by the natural light of reason, and the truth of faith known through divine revelation.

The sheer volume of his written work is amazing; the best-known of his books is the *Summa Theologiae*, which he left unfinished when he died. It is divided into three parts, and begins with the nature of theology, the existence and nature of God in his Unity and in the Trinity, and his attributes; next he deals with creation, with God as the End of creatures and the total dependence of creatures on the Creator; then with the analogical nature of our knowledge of God. The second part deals with the Angels, human nature, the spiritual activity of man, happiness, grace and the virtues. The third part treats of Christ as our Redeemer and Way to God, the hypostatic union and the Sacraments. The deep penetration of Saint Thomas into everything he discusses marks him as the greatest of scholars, philosophers and theologians. The secret of his greatness is without doubt his sanctity. His writings concerning the Blessed Sacrament are a proof of his immense love for Jesus Christ present in the Sacred Species. During the time he was composing the third part of the Summa he was seen by the sacristan praying before an image of the Crucified Christ. The sacristan saw Saint Thomas raised from the ground and heard a voice from the figure of Christ say to him, *You have written well of me, Thomas, what reward would you have of me?* The reply was, *Nothing other than Thyself, Lord!*

Love of the Blessed Sacrament and of Our Lady

Thanks to the request of Saint Thomas, the feast of Corpus Christi was extended to the universal Church by Pope Urban IV, who entrusted him with the task of composing the office for the feast, which includes the *Lauda Sion*, *O Salutaris*, and *Pange lingua*, which finishes with the *Tantum ergo*. The beautiful hymn

Adoro Te devote, (O Godhead hid, devoutly I adore Thee), is also his work, as well as some prayers for before and after Holy Communion. Saint Thomas had a very deep devotion to Our Lady; his confessor, Father Reginald of Piperno, says that he never asked anything through the intercession of Our Lady without receiving it. One Lent he preached a series of sermons just on the words *Ave Maria*, and these same words were found written time and time again in the margin of an autographed copy of the *Summa contra Gentiles*. Another of his brief but beautiful prayers to Our Lady asks, *O Virgin full of goodness, obtain for me the grace of loving your Son, my Saviour Jesus Christ, with a true and perfect love, and, after him, of loving you with my whole heart.*

The last journey

His writing came to an abrupt end on the 6th of December 1273, the feast of Saint Nicholas. Since he seemed to be exhausted from overwork, he was sent with Fr Reginald to rest in the castle of San Severino, which belonged to his sister Theodora. He remained there a month, with no change. On his return to Naples, Fr Reginald again asked him to continue to write. Saint Thomas told him, *I cannot. After what God has revealed to me all that I have written seems as straw.* He was still unwell when the request came from the Pope for him to attend the General Council of Lyons for the reunion of the Greeks with Rome. Saint Thomas set out from Naples accompanied by Fr Reginald, but became so seriously ill that he was taken to the nearest monastery, that of the Cistercians in Fossa Nuova. He went first to visit the Blessed Sacrament, then the monks took him to the room of the Abbot, where they took care of him. At the request of these monks he dictated for them a commentary on the Canticle of Canticles. When he became weaker, he requested the Holy Viaticum and Anointing of the sick, which he received with great devotion. He died on the 7th of March 1274, conscious to the end, with great peace and full of love of God. He was canonized by Pope John XXII in 1323, and chosen as Patron of all Catholic universities, colleges and schools by Pope Leo XIII.

The perennial value of his philosophy and theology has been insisted upon by the Popes up to the present day; it is to be used as a basis for studies in seminaries and similar academic institutions, being the best vehicle for transmitting the truths of philosophy and theology in accordance with the mind of the Church.

Saint Thomas More

Saint Thomas More was born on the 6th of February 1478 in London. His father, Sir John More, was a lawyer and later became a judge. His mother, Agnes, died when Thomas was four years old, leaving Sir John with six young children. Thomas began his education at Saint Anthony's school, which was attached to a hospital of the same name, and later went as a page in the household of Cardinal Morton, the Archbishop of Canterbury, whose residence was in Lambeth Palace near the river Thames. The elderly Cardinal noticed the lively intelligence of the boy and commented to one of his friends, *This child here waiting at table, whoever shall live to see it, will prove a marvellous man...*

Lawyer and humanist

The Cardinal sent him to Canterbury College, Oxford (now part of Christ Church), when he was fourteen. He was there for two years studying literature and philosophy, and remembers that his father allowed him very little money, for which he was very grateful in retrospect, as in this way he had learned *a certain detachment* from material goods. Sir John wanted his son to become a lawyer like himself and arranged for him to continue his studies at the Inns of Court in London, where he qualified as a barrister in 1501. He never lost his enthusiasm for literature, and with Linacre, Colet, Grocyn and Lilly became fluent in both Greek and Latin and was considered one of the foremost scholars of his time. That same year the heir to the throne, Prince Arthur, married Catherine, daughter of the King and Queen of Spain. Thomas was endeavouring to discover his vocation in life and spent some time as a guest in the London Charterhouse, continuing his studies there and joining in the prayers of the monks. Colet, his friend and spiritual director, introduced him to the writings of the Fathers of the Church, in particular to those of Saint Augustine. Thomas delivered a series of widely acclaimed lectures on this saint in Saint Lawrence's church. With Colet's help he decided to seek his way of sanctity in his profession as a lawyer and man of letters, remaining in the world and carrying out his work for the glory of God.

Married life

In 1504 he was elected Member of Parliament, and the following year married Jane Colt, one of a family of three sisters. His son-in-law, William Roper, gives a touching insight into Thomas' concern for others: *Albeit his mind most served him to the second daughter, for that he thought her the fairest and best favoured, yet when he considered it could be both great grief and some shame also to the eldest to see her younger sister in marriage preferred before her, he then of a certain pity framed his fancy toward her and soon after married her.* His choice was well made; the couple, who had three daughters and a son, were very happy together. Thomas passed on his love of music and literature to his young wife, who was eager to learn. Jane died when the eldest child was six. Thomas married for a second time, a widow, Alice Middleton, who had a daughter of the same name. More's second wife was very efficient and a kind mother to his children. The household, which also included Alice's daughter, other children whom More took in, and later his son and daughter-in-law and all the grandchildren, was a true example of Christian family life. More's great friend Erasmus, the great scholar from Rotterdam, described in a letter the home he so much delighted to visit. *With what gentleness does my friend regulate his household, where misunderstandings and quarrels are altogether unknown! Indeed he is looked up to as a general healer of all differences, and was never known to part from any on terms of unkindness. His house seems to enjoy the peculiar happiness that all who dwell under its roof go forth into the world bettered in their morals, as well as improved in their condition; and no spot was ever known to fall on the reputation of any of its fortunate inhabitants. Here you might imagine yourself in the academy of Plato. But indeed I should do injustice to his house by comparing it with the school of that philosopher, where nothing but abstract questions, and occasionally moral virtues, were the subjects of discussion; it would be truer to call it a school of religion and an arena for the exercise of all the Christian virtues. All its inmates apply themselves to liberal studies, though piety is their first care. No wrangling or angry word is ever heard within the walls. No-one is idle; everyone does his duty with alacrity, and regularity and good order are prescribed by the mere force of kindness and courtesy. Everyone performs his allotted task and yet all are as cheerful as if mirth were their only employment. Surely such a household deserves to be called a school of the Christian religion ... with his wife, son and daughter-in-law, his three daughters and their husbands, with eleven grand-children. There is not any man alive so loving to his children as he; and such is the excellence of his temper that when anything happens which cannot be helped he takes it as if nothing could have chanced more happily.*

Affairs of State

More made numerous close friends in England as well as in Europe, where he travelled on more than one occasion – to Flanders, for example, on a commercial embassy in 1515 (it was there that he wrote his *Utopia*) and again in 1517. His skill attracted the attention of Cardinal Wolsey and King Henry VIII, who had succeeded his father Henry VII since his brother Arthur had died soon after his marriage to Princess Catherine. More was appointed to the King's Council and soon won the esteem of Henry and his Queen. With a papal dispension, requested by Henry VII, Henry had married his brother's widow. More had accepted this post reluctantly, as it meant separation from his wife and family, but he continued to supervise the education of his children, treating his daughters in exactly the same way as his son, which was unusual at that time, as it was generally considered a waste to educate girls. His correspondence with the children was carried out in Latin; Margaret, his eldest, made particularly good progress in her studies.

Promotion for Thomas came rapidly. In 1518 he was made Master of the Court of Requests, accompanied the King to the *Field of Cloth of Gold* in 1520, and became Under-Treasurer in 1521, when he also received a knighthood. The post of Speaker of the House of Commons followed in 1523; two years later he became Chancellor of the Duchy of Lancaster. Despite all his official duties, Sir Thomas spent as much time as possible with his family, which had moved from the centre of London to a large house in Chelsea. He also pursued his interest in his own studies. He wrote among other things a treatise on the Four Last Things and, with Erasmus, a Latin translation of Lucian from the Greek, a life of Pico della

Mirandola the Italian scholar, and a life of Richard III.
King Henry VIII produced his *Defence of the Seven
Sacraments* against the errors of Martin Luther and
asked More's opinion on it. More suggested that
perhaps too much emphasis was given to the Temporal
power of the papacy, but Henry insisted that it remain
as he had written it, saying that he owed his crown to
the Holy See. In recognition for this book the King was
given by the Pope the title of Fidei Defensor (Defender
of the Faith) – a title which British monarchs still
retain and which to this day appears on coins of the
realm. Sir Thomas wrote a reply to Luther in Latin,
then, in accordance with the wishes of Bishop Tunstal,
a series of writings in English refuting the German
friar's heresies and defending Catholic doctrine. This
demanded much study and work, for as More said, *It is
easier and quicker to write heresies than to repudiate
them adequately.*

The Royal Succession

Luther's heresies were not the only cause for concern to Henry and his subjects. Henry wanted a male
heir; after eleven years of marriage to Catherine, the
only child to survive was a daughter, Mary. He was also
very attracted by one of the Queen's ladies-in-waiting
– Anne Boleyn. Henry sought a solution by demanding
a declaration that his marriage to Catherine was
invalid, as she had previously been his brother's wife.
Cardinal Wolsey, Lord Chancellor of England, was
given the task of obtaining the dispensation. The opinions of the universities in England and abroad were
asked, and that of Sir Thomas More. He told Henry
that as a layman he was not competent to express an
opinion on a matter pertaining to the ecclesiastical
authority and, at first, the King appeared to respect his

views, telling More that he should not act against his conscience and that he *should first look unto God and after God unto him*. Wolsey proved unsuccessful in fulfilling his royal master's desires and was deprived of his position as Chancellor. In 1529 Henry bestowed the chain of office on Sir Thomas More, hoping in this way to obtain his cooperation, much as his namesake, Henry II, had done in making Saint Thomas à Becket his Chancellor. More performed his duties as Lord Chancellor with such diligence that, for the first – and last – time, there were no pending cases to be dealt with.

By 1531 Henry was becoming impatient at the delay in obtaining the divorce from Catherine, who had stated under oath that her marriage with Arthur had not been consummated, this being one of the grounds on which the original dispensation for her to marry Henry had been granted. An Act of Submission was drawn up, to be accepted by Parliament and the clergy, granting the King legislative authority in ecclesiastical matters. More had done all he could to prevent approval of the Act, but without success. The clergy capitulated on the 15th of May 1532, with the exception of the Bishop of Rochester, John Fisher. Sir Thomas More resigned as Lord Chancellor. His family could not understand why he had given up a position of such prestige, thus losing his means of livelihood, when almost everyone else of importance had consented to the King's will. More returned to his studies and his writings, refusing to be drawn to express an opinion on *the King's Proceedings*.

Matters moved swiftly in 1533. Henry and Anne Boleyn were married secretly in January, two months before the new Archbishop of Canterbury, Thomas Cranmer, had at Henry's instigation declared the marriage to Catherine invalid. Anne was crowned Queen in June of the same year; she deeply resented the fact that Sir Thomas More refused to attend the coronation. In March 1534 the long-awaited reply came from Rome – the Pope stated that Henry's marriage to Catherine was valid. Parliament hastily approved the Act of Succession granting power to the King to enforce all its contents. More was ordered to appear at Lambeth Palace on the 13th of April to swear to the Act and therefore give his agreement to the King's new *marriage*.

After going to Confession, Mass and Holy Communion, Sir Thomas set off for Lambeth, where he indicated that he had no objection to swearing to accept whatever referred to the rights of succession, as this could be determined by the King and Parliament; but he refused to say anything which was against the authority of the Pope. Bishop John Fisher was summoned on the same day. They were given a few days to reconsider their replies, and as both remained adamant they were sent as prisoners to the Tower of London. At the end of 1534 Acts of Attainder were passed on each of them, condemning them to life imprisonment and confiscation of their property. Some of Sir Thomas' lands were given to Anne Boleyn's family.

Arrests and executions

Parliament then passed a new Act of Treason, making it a capital offence to attempt in any way to *deprive the King and his heirs of their dignity, title, or name of their Royal Estates*. The earlier Act of Supremacy had given the King and his heirs the title of Supreme Head of the Church of England.

Bishop Fisher and Sir Thomas were subjected to interrogations and efforts to convince them to take the oath. More's family was allowed to visit him and at first he had the use of his books and writing materials. Finally he was deprived of these. During his fifteen-month imprisonment he had written a *Dialogue of Comfort in Tribulation*, and a work on the Passion of Our Lord, which he was unable to finish.

On the 4th of May the three imprisoned Carthusian priors, a secular priest and a Bridgettine monk were led out, where Sir Thomas could see them, to be dragged on hurdles to Tyburn, the first of hundreds to die under the Act of Supremacy, for refusing to deny the Catholic faith. Far from terrifying More, this made him wish for the grace to follow in their footsteps.

It was becoming more and more important to the King to have the agreement of the Bishop of Rochester and the one-time Lord Chancellor, because of the esteem in which they were held. The Pope created Bishop Fisher a Cardinal, hoping that the king would relent, but the comment of Henry was that *the Pope could send him the red hat if he wished, but I shall see that he has no head to wear it.* Cardinal Fisher was condemned for speaking against the King's title on the 17th of June and executed on the 22nd.

Sir Thomas More's trial was on the 1st of July in Westminster Hall, where More had exercised his office as Judge on many occasions. Weak from his imprisonment, he was provided with a chair whilst the lengthy accusation was made against him. More made a very able defence, until a perjured witness, Richard Rich, swore that Sir Thomas had denied the King's title in a conversation with him in the Tower. Sir Thomas pointed out that he would be very unlikely to confide in Rich, knowing his reputation, when he had confided in no-one else. *And if this oath of yours, Mr Rich, be true, then pray I that I may never see God face to face, which*

I would not say, were it otherwise, to win the whole world. More then repeated the conversation he had had with Rich in the Tower and concluded, *In faith, Mr Rich, I am sorrier for your perjury than for mine own peril.*

The pre-arranged verdict of Guilty was given. More then spoke freely and explained how no layman could be head of Christ's Church. The sentence for treachery was passed – he was to be dragged on a hurdle to the place of execution and there be hanged, drawn and quartered. Sir Thomas's reply was typical of him: *As the blessed Apostle Paul was present and consented to the death of Saint Stephen, and yet be they now both twain holy Saints in Heaven, so I very trust and shall therefore right heartily pray, that though your Lordships have now in earth been judges to my condemnation, we may yet hereafter in Heaven merrily all meet together to our everlasting salvation..*

Leading him back to the Tower, the Constable wept, as did many of the bystanders when his son knelt before him to ask his blessing, and his daughter too pushed through the guards to embrace her father. He spent his remaining days in the Tower praying and preparing for his death, still not knowing when it would come. On the 5th of July he wrote a letter with charcoal to Margaret, which finished, *Farewell, my dear child, and pray for me and I shall for you and all your friends, that we may merrily meet in Heaven.* He also sent her the rough hair-shirt he had always worn, even in prison.

On the morning of the 6th of July he was told he was to die that day. The King had previously sent a message that as a favour he would be beheaded on Tower Hill. Saint Thomas remarked, *God keep my friends from such favours!* He had been forbidden to make the customary speech before his execution, so requested the prayers of all present and said, *I die the King's good servant, but God's first*. He joked with the Lieutenant, *See me safe up, I pray you; at my coming down, let me shift for myself*. He then knelt and prayed Psalm 50, the *Miserere*, gave the executioner some money and embraced him, then laid his head on the block.

His body was buried on Tower Hill, in a common grave, and his head displayed on a spike on London Bridge. Margaret bribed the executioner to give it to her and it is now buried in the Roper vault in Saint Dunstan's church, Canterbury, together with the remains of his beloved daughter.

He was beatified in 1886 with John Fisher and many others of the martyrs, and canonized in 1935, the fourth centenary of his martyrdom. His feast is now celebrated on the 22nd of June in conjunction with that of Saint John Fisher.